The Weider Book of Bodybuilding for Women

The Weider Book of Bodybuilding for Women

Betty Weider & Joe Weider

Contemporary Books, Inc.
Chicago

Library of Congress Cataloging in Publication Data

Weider, Betty.
The Weider book of bodybuilding for women.

Bibliography: p.
Includes index.
1. Bodybuilding for women. I. Weider, Joe.
II. Title.
GV546.6.W64W44 646.7′5 81-65195
ISBN 0-8092-5907-9 AACR2
ISBN 0-8092-5906-0 (pbk.)

Exercises posed by Cassandra Gava and Carla Hogendeyk.
Photographed by Peter Brenner.

Exercises photographed principally at Gold's Gym, Venice, California. Nautilus exercises photographed at Nautilus of California, Inc., Woodland Hills, California.

All other photos courtesy of the International Federation of Bodybuilders.

Published by Contemporary Books, Inc.
180 North Michigan Avenue, Chicago, Illinois 60601
Manufactured in the United States of America
Library of Congress Catalog Card Number: 81-65195
International Standard Book Number: 0-8092-5907-9 (cloth)
0-8092-5906-0 (paper)

Published simultaneously in Canada by
Beaverbooks, Ltd.
150 Lesmill Road
Don Mills, Ontario M3B 2T5
Canada

Contents

1

Weight Training and Bodybuilding

Weight training and bodybuilding are fabulous activities for any woman!

By training with weights and adopting better nutritional habits you can literally change your life 100 percent for the better. You can totally reshape your body by firming flabby hips, legs, and arms or by building up and shaping any part of your body that is skinny. You can actually sculpt your body to look like anything your heart desires.

If you are serious about participating in any sport, you can markedly improve your abilities in it through weight training. Of all those components that come together to make a successful athlete—strength, aerobic fitness, flexibility, skill, mental preparedness, quick reaction time, etc.—strength is the easiest to improve. And when your strength has been increased, you will notice a quantum jump in your athletic performance ability.

Due to your ability to zero in on individual muscle groups with weight-training exercises, you will find that you can quickly rehabilitate any injured area of your body with resistance training. It is only through weight training that injured athletes are able to return to high-level competition as quickly as they do today

Regardless of the goal a woman pursues via weight training, she will receive the incidental benefit of improved health and physical fitness. And when she also watches her diet, she can accentuate these benefits. After only two or three weeks of weight training and healthy eating you will have developed an almost unbelievable sense of well-being. In fact, you will begin to feel so good that you will soon find yourself positively addicted to regular, weight-training workouts.

Some women become so involved with reshaping their bodies and improving their self-image through weight training that they eventually decide to enter bodybuilding competition. This type of competition can be very rewarding, both personally and financially. Many women bodybuilders are now even able to make a living from professional bodybuilding.

Despite the goal you decide to pursue through weight training, *you* are totally in control of the results you receive. No one else can train or diet for you. Only you can discipline yourself to work out regularly, and only you can avoid progress-halting junk foods. But when you do it right, you can take your mind and body to incredible heights of fitness *totally on your own.*

Age and initial physical condition are no barriers to progress through weight training. From ten to a hundred years of age, you can make tremendous progress from your weight workouts, although women over fifty will probably progress more slowly than younger women. And regardless of how fat or out of shape you are, you can match an initial level of training intensity to your physical condition. Then you can slowly increase the intensity of your workouts until after a few months you can work out as hard as any woman.

The beauty of weight training lies in the fact that you *can* do it. Any woman can achieve undreamed-of results simply by training regularly with weights and watching her diet. You, too, can do it, so let's don a pair of shorts and a T-shirt and hit the weights!

CASE HISTORIES

Every woman who has taken up weight training and stuck with it has a success story that would inspire you to take up the activity yourself. In this section of Chapter 1, we will present four such case histories of women weight trainers who will inspire you to either begin or continue with your own progressive weight-training program.

Stacey Bentley

"I hope that every fat girl out there decides she's had enough and that it's time to make a change," Stacey Bentley exclaims. "It can be done, and I'm a good example of what weight training can do for any woman. I was the most insecure and fat teenager you could imagine. At 5′1″ in height, I seldom weighed as little as 140 pounds, and my bathroom scale occasionally shocked me by revealing a big 150 on its dial.

"I was reluctant to express an opinion on anything, and I thought that anyone who was nice to me was just doing me a favor. My excuse for every failure was that I was fat. If I didn't get a job or wasn't chosen for some activity, it was just because I was fat. And this led to a vicious cycle in which I ate even more and became even fatter to compensate for my self-doubts and failures.

"Then at age eighteen I discovered weight training. Within a year of training and sensible dieting, I had lost 30 pounds—from 145 to 115 pounds—and greatly improved my self-image. After another year I was down to 105 and looked absolutely fabulous. I even decided to enter bodybuilding competitions and won several titles!"

By her sterling example, Stacey Bentley believes that she can encourage and inspire other women to take up serious weight training. "It's sometimes an uphill battle, however," she confesses, "since many women are still fighting the myths and misinformation about their bodies that they've been taught all of their lives. But times are changing, and ultimately weight training will be as popular with women as jogging now is."

"Fat women *can* improve, and I've shown that," Stacey concludes. "It takes time and effort, but it's so much better than putting up with the anxieties and insecurities of being fat and badly out of shape. I hope that every woman can learn to understand this, because weight training and a healthy diet can totally change their lives!"

Stacey Bentley, winner of numerous bodybuilding titles both in single competition and in mixed doubles competition.

Cindy Carlson

Cindy Carlson is a very busy woman. At 28 years of age, she manages a large store, is working on a Master's degree in business administration, and even has time for a full social life.

The secret of Cindy's vitality is her approach to regular exercise and healthy dietary practices. She has found that she has far more energy for her nonstop days if she either weight trains, jogs, or plays tennis 30 minutes or more per day and follows a limited-calorie diet consisting of fresh, health-promoting foods.

"My boyfriend introduced me to weight training, and we now work out together three days per week in a gym," Cindy told us recently. "It really enhances our relationship, because he's as busy as I am and it's difficult for us to find time to spend together. But we are both hooked on a physical fitness life-style, and since we'd work out anyway, we do our weight training and jogging—plus play tennis on weekends—together. We both totally enjoy this time that we spend together!"

Interestingly, Cindy Carlson has found that regular exercise has had a tremendously positive effect on her mind as well as on her body. "Originally, I took up jogging to reduce my overweight body from 150 pounds down to 120," she told us. "But now I'd keep my weight training and jogging up even if it didn't help keep my weight under control. That's because regular exercise clears away all of the cobwebs that used to cloud my mind at work or when I was studying. Now my mind is totally clear, and it operates at peak efficiency during all of my waking hours."

P.S. Cindy is a *summa cum laude* graduate of California State University at Northridge, as well as a straight "A" student in her M.B.A. program.

Patricia Loverock

Patricia Loverock ran the 100- and 200-meter dashes internationally on the track teams of her native Canada. She has won numerous national championships, and in 1976 she was a member of the Canadian Olympic team, one of the greatest honors an athlete can receive. And Patricia credits regular weight-training workouts for much of her athletic success.

"Sprinting speed is directly related to the strength of the thigh and calf muscles," she told us as we were preparing this book. "Once I started regular weight-training workouts, I noticed a quick and significant reduction in my times. That hooked me, and I weight trained for the rest of my competitive days."

Now retired from track and field competition, married, and having recently completed a Master's degree in journalism, Patricia Loverock

Weight-training workouts made a significant difference in Patricia Loverock's running times. Combined with running, weight training is an essential way to keep healthy and fit.

works as an editor for our magazines, *Shape* and *Muscle & Fitness*. And she still weight trains regularly. "Combined with running, weight training gives me an optimum degree of health and physical fitness," she said. "There's no better way to remain lean, fit, and youthful looking."

Tanya Harrison

Since she has four young children, 30-year-old Tanya Harrison has a certain degree of difficulty finding any time for herself. "But I always *make* time for a 30-minute weight workout five or six days per week," she says enthusiastically. "These workouts not only keep me in good shape, but they are the one thing I most look forward to every day. They're my own personal and private time, and without them I might never survive. Even if the kids were burning the house down around my ears, I'd never miss a workout nor stop once I'd started it."

Tanya Harrison is also one of the thousands of overly thin women who have normalized their body weight through weight training and a high-calorie diet. At 5′8″ in height, she once weighed only 100 pounds, while today she weighs a healthy 130 pounds and has a sensational figure!

MYTH AND REALITY

Unfortunately, many a woman is dissuaded from weight training by a well-meaning—but ill-informed—friend who tells her she will become masculine looking, muscle-bound, or badly injured by weight training. Why such myths continue is beyond our comprehension, but they do, and they should be corrected by the following explanations of why each commonly believed myth is totally untrue.

1. *Weight training will make you look like a man.* Because women have very low levels of

the male muscle-building hormone testosterone in their bodies, it is impossible for them to build the massive muscles of a man. In point of fact, few women can build much appreciable muscle mass, and then they can do so only through the heaviest and hardest workouts imaginable. In reality, any muscle tissue a woman—including you—might develop will show up on her body only as feminine curves.

2. *Weight training will make you slow and muscle-bound.* Innumerable scientific studies have proven beyond a doubt that weight training enhances both speed of movement and body flexibility. If weight training harmed either speed or flexibility, there wouldn't be so many women athletes using hard-weight workouts to improve their performance in sports.

3. *All of your muscle will turn to fat once you stop weight training.* It is physiologically impossible for muscle to turn to fat in the human body. Any muscle tissue you develop through weight training will merely shrink back to its original size once you stop working out. And unless you consistently overeat, you will not get fat once you stop working out with weights.

4. *You'll get a hernia or hurt your back lifting weights.* Very few women are injured while training with weights as long as they warm up carefully before a workout, stay warm while training, and use the correct body mechanics outlined for each exercise described and illustrated in this book. In reality, weight training actually prevents injuries, including hernia and back problems.

5. *Weight training will stunt your growth and ruin your sex life.* Actually any form of regular exercise—weight training included—will stimulate growth in stature. Any physically fit woman will find her sex life greatly improved over what it was when she was out of shape. And as a bonus she'll find all of her menstrual problems either eliminated or greatly reduced.

HOW TO USE THIS BOOK

The rest of this book is divided into five chapters, a glossary, and an appendix. In Chapter 2 we will teach you the basic essentials of weight training, the techniques you will use at the beginning level, as well as for the rest of your weight-training involvement. This basic information is then complemented in Chapter 3 by a beginning exercise pool and several beginning-level training programs that you should try. If you have less than two or three months of training experience, the advice and workouts in Chapters 2 and 3 will be most appropriate for you.

Chapters 4 and 5 give you intermediate and advanced training tips, exercises and workouts. So if you have been training for more than two or three months, read these two chapters, and then choose the training routines most appropriate for your unique goals and weight-training experience level. There are a number of progressively more difficult workouts listed in Chapter 5.

Chapter 6 is devoted to a discussion of women's competitive bodybuilding, the most advanced form of weight training for women. While this activity will appeal only to a minor percentage of women, anyone who elects to become a competitive bodybuilder will thrive on the supremely dedicated life-style it demands.

Following Chapter 6 are a glossary and an appendix. The glossary defines the main weight-training and bodybuilding terms, so consult it immediately if you encounter some type of weight-training jargon with which you are unfamiliar while either reading this book or working out in a gym.

In the appendix at the end of this book are answers to the 20 questions that women most frequently ask us about weight training and bodybuilding. Perhaps these are questions that you, too, have had, so be sure to read the appendix for answers to your questions before you go much farther in this book.

Your best bet will probably be to read this entire book quickly to locate the levels at which you should start. Then go back and read more carefully the sections most applicable to you

ONWARD

In the next chapter we will provide you with all of the basic training tips that you will need to understand before taking a workout with the exercises and training routines listed in Chapter 3. So, let's get down to basics and begin to learn the correct way to weight train!

2

Beginning Training Techniques

In this chapter we will teach you a series of basic weight-training techniques that you will use for as long as you work out with weights. The topics covered in the chapter include the importance of a physical exam, basic weight-training terminology, where to train, an equipment orientation, time factors, progression, muscle physiology, basic nutrition, sleep and rest, what to wear, break-in and muscle soreness, warm-ups, safety, the value of strict exercise form, and proper breathing.

PHYSICAL EXAMINATION

If you are over 30 years of age and have been physically inactive in recent years, we strongly recommend that you schedule a complete physical examination with your family physician. If you are past 40, this examination should also include a stress test electrocardiogram (EKG).

As you become older or if you have been out of good physical condition for a long period of time, your body can fall prey to various diseases and health irregularities that could endanger your well-being during periods of heavy physical exercise. A complete physical exam is the only way to detect such health hazzards.

PROGESS SLOWLY

One of the biggest temptations—particularly for men—when starting a program of regular exercise is to try to regain one's youth almost overnight. Instead of progressing slowly and sensibly in their workouts, many men and women go totally overboard, trying to make up for years of physical neglect with a few days of all-out exercise.

Unfortunately, the human body—once it is out of shape—rebels at exercise, becoming so sore that most would-be bodybuilders throw their hands up in disgust after only a few days of torturous workouts. "Hey, this hurts!" they say to themselves. "I'm not going to hurt *myself!*"

If you've been physically inactive for more than a year, you should begin your weight training at a very low intensity level and then progress very slowly, allowing your body to adapt gradually to the new stresses you're putting on it. The rate at which you can progress safely will vary according to how long you've been inactive, so listen closely to your body as you move from workout to workout. If you feel unduly fatigued or overly stressed, simply slow your pace a bit.

BASIC TERMINOLOGY

The jargon of weight training and bodybuilding will seem bewildering to many beginning trainees, so in this section we will explain the meaning of every key weight-training term. You can also refer to the glossary at the back of this book for additional definitions.

Let's start with the meaning of weight training and bodybuilding. *Weight training* is a general term to indicate working out with weights for any number of purposes—to improve sports performance, to attain better health, to reshape the body, to rehabilitate an injury, etc. *Bodybuilding* lies within the realm of weight training. It is working out with weights specifically to reshape the body.

The words *exercise* and *movement* are interchangeable, and both refer to the individual movements you do when training (i.e., a Pushup or its barbell equivalent, a Bench Press). By doing a number of different exercises in one session, you have completed a *workout*, also variously called a *training session*, a *routine*, and a *program*.

When you actually do an excerise, each individual complete movement of that exercise is called a *repetition* or, more commonly, a *rep*. And a group of reps (usually 8 to 12) is called a *set*. After doing a set, we take a *rest interval* of about 60 seconds (occasionally called simply a *rest between sets*) and then do another set or even several more.

WHERE TO TRAIN

There are a myriad of places you can actually train, and each has its advantages and disadvantages. The most convenient place will be at home, because there you will have complete privacy, as well as total access to equipment, regardless of the hour of the day.

At the beginning level, you will need only a 100-pound adjustable barbell and dumbbell set, plus an adjustable exercise bench. This equipment will cost approximately $150.00 new, but that's a one-time investment, as opposed to yearly dues at a gym or health club.

The best place to train at home will be in a garage or basement, where you can set aside a special area for your workouts. But you can train anywhere in your home or apartment that you can find an area free of furniture and measuring about 5′ × 5′.

Weight rooms at most high schools and colleges have been open to both women and men for the past few years. Most are well-equipped and closely supervised. Plus, when men and women train together, they usually find some excellent social opportunities.

YMCA weight rooms are about equal in quality to those of a high school or college, but with the added expense of a YMCA membership required. Some YMCAs have much better weight rooms than others, so be sure to shop around.

Health spas generally have excellent facilities—particularly in such amenities as saunas, jacuzzis, indoor swimming pools, and well-chromed weights—but the cost of a membership at a spa can be humungous. A year's membership averages about $400, which would buy you a wide variety of home gym exercise equipment. And, we've noticed that some spa instructors discourage women who train hard on the theory that seeing perspiration on the brow of a woman can frighten off potential members.

Nautilus facilities are also very expensive, and at most you are limited to training exclusively with Nautilus machines. Few have any free weights (barbells and dumbbells) available. Nautilus machines offer high-intensity resistance training, but the number of exercises that you can do on the machines is severely limited. We prefer the greater variety offered by free weights.

The final—and by far the best—place to train is a commercial bodybuilding gym, most of which now encourage women to join their membership. These gyms vary widely in the variety of equipment they have, but if you can find a big one like the famous Gold's Gym in Venice, California, or the World Gym in Santa Monica, California, you'll be able to train with all three major forms of resistance equipment—free weights, Universal Gyms, and Nautilus machines. (See the next section of this chapter for an equipment orientation.) Nothing can beat training with all three types of equipment!

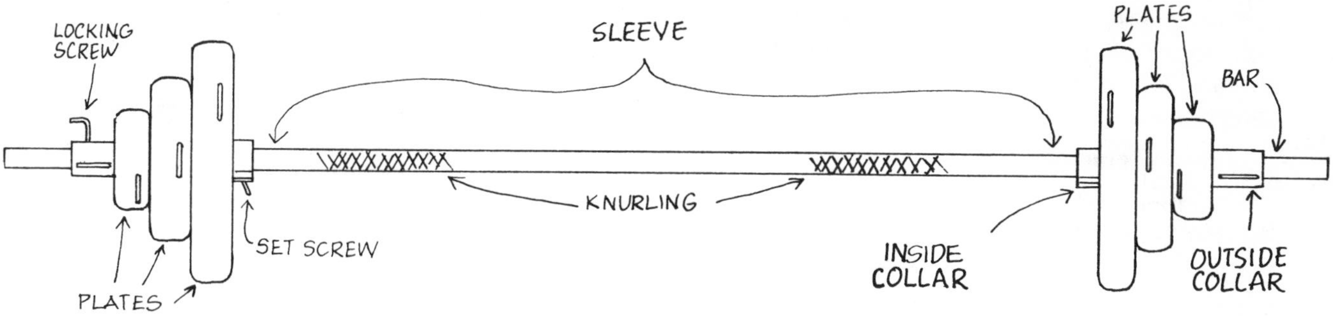

EQUIPMENT ORIENTATION

As just mentioned, there are three major types of resistance-training equipment—free weights, Universal Gyms, and Nautilus machines. Let's discuss each of these types of equipment.

Free Weights

Barbells have been in common use since the mid-1800s, although they were unwieldly solid iron weights, not the modern adjustable sets we use. And dumbbells—which are merely short-handled barbells—have been in existence for nearly as long.

Each part of an adjustable barbell or dumbbell has a name. So you won't be embarrassed if someone asks you for a "collar" or a "plate," see the illustration of a barbell with its various parts labeled.

The basic bar is made of steel and is either four, five, or six feet in length. Normally, a hollow tube called a sleeve is slipped over the bar to make it easier for the bar to revolve in your hands as you train. Knurlings are grooves scored into the sleeve, so your grip will remain secure when your hands perspire. The inside and outside collars keep the plates in position as you use your barbell and dumbbells.

Plates come in sizes ranging from 1¼ pounds up through 100 pounds. They are made either of cast iron or of concrete covered by vinyl. The vinyl-covered plates are the most popular at the present time. Cast-iron plates are far more durable than the vinyl-covered ones, and you can put more of them on a bar, because they're thinner than concrete plates. On the other hand, the vinyl plates are much easier on rugs and floors if you have to train in your living room or bedroom.

If you train in a large, well-organized gym, you'll have the luxury of training with *fixed weights,* or barbells and dumbbells with the plates locked or welded permanently into position on the bar. This, of course, requires a large number of barbells and dumbbells to provide a sufficient range of weights; hence the reason these fixed weights are usually available only in large commercial gyms.

A large variety of benches, racks, pulleys, and bars have evolved for use with free weights. For a beginner, there is such a bewildering array of equipment that we will explain the use of each piece as we describe the exercises using free weights in Chapters 3 and 5.

Universal Gyms

Universal Gyms became popular during the late 1960s, primarily because one gym offers exercises for every muscle group and can accommodate six to ten trainees at one time. Because of their convenience, Universal Gyms are quite popular with institutions like high schools, military bases, and YMCAs. But the high cost of a Universal Gym (up to $5000) makes the machine impractical for home-gym use.

The weakness of Universal Gyms is in the variety of exercises that can be done on one. Only one movement is available for some muscle groups, and no body part has more than six to eight exercises that can be done for it on a Universal Gym. In contrast, literally hundreds of movements can be done for most body parts with free weights. Since lack of variety leads to boredom in weight training, this is a serious drawback. Still, when used in combination with free weights, the Universal Gym is an excellent piece of equipment.

Nautilus Machines

Nautilus machines first made an impact on weight training at the beginning of the 1970s, and by 1980 they had become popular. Nautilus machines are based on sound biomechanical and physiological principles. In fact, they are based on the time-tested Weider System of training, which has been in common use for 30 years. Thus, the machines will give you an excellent workout, particularly when used in conjunction with barbells and dumbbells.

There are, however, three major drawbacks to Nautilus training. The first of these is the expense. The machines cost $3000 to $5000 each, and a complete enough installation to allow you to train every muscle group thoroughly would cost in the neighborhood of $50,000! Even the cost of a year's membership at a Nautilus facility is pretty stiff (averaging $300 to $350 per year).

The second disadvantage is shared with Universal Gyms. This is the lack of variety of exercises that you can do with Nautilus machines as compared to free weights. As a result, we have heard compaints from many women that Nautilus training is boring.

The final disadvantage is the type of advertising Nautilus facilities use. Typically, they claim that a three-times-a-week 20-minute workout is sufficient to develop optimum strength, cardiorespiratory fitness, and muscle mass. This is totally false! And when a woman believes such a sales pitch, she is cheating herself of half the results she could achieve with free weights.

TIME FACTORS

There are a number of temporal factors to be considered in weight training and bodybuilding. You should be totally familiar with each time factor before you even *think* about touching a weight.

When to Train

The only important thing to consider about when to train is finding a time of the day when you can *always* do your workouts free of distractions. This is important because the human body thrives on regularity and will begin to peak its energy reserves for a certain time of the day if that is when the workout is always done.

We have known women who train at every hour of the day. The choice of this hour depends more on whether you are a "morning person" or a "night person," since it will be most comfortable to train when you are feeling at your best.

How Long to Train

The basic workouts in Chapter 3 should take only about 20 minutes to complete, and most of the routines in this book can be finished in less than an hour. Even a high-level competitive bodybuilder will put in no more than one-and-a-half hours for each workout. So if you find yourself training longer than an hour, you are either doing too many total sets, training too slowly, or talking too much between sets.

How Many Days per Week

At the beginning level, you should train three nonconsecutive days per week. Most commonly, women train on Mondays, Wednesdays, and Fridays, but any other days of the week are equally as good, as long as you have a rest day between each training day. A muscle will need 48 hours to recuperate between workouts, so training a muscle group two days in a row will actually retard your progress.

When you've reached the advanced training level, you'll be able to train four to six days per week. Still, each muscle group will be trained only two or three times per week, since only part of the body is worked each day, and the parts are rotated during the week.

Rest Between Sets

To build the greatest degree of muscle mass and strength we will do several consecutive sets of each exercise, with a rest interval between each set. This rest interval averages between 30 and 90 seconds, with 60 seconds being the most common. If you rest more than 90 seconds between sets your body will tend to cool off, which makes you more vulnerable to injury.

When Not to Work Out

Never train any muscle group with weights on

a scheduled rest day. And never train when you are ill. Other than those exceptions, throw 100 percent effort into your workouts every training day, and you'll soon be surprised at the progress you're making.

PROGRESSION

Progression is the heart of bodybuilding and weight training, because muscles grow as a result of having progressively heavier resistance placed on them. Let's say that your right frontal thigh muscle is normally capable of doing 100 arbitrary units of work. If you place 101 units of stress on this muscle, that extra stress will *feel* heavy. But the muscle will adapt by growing stronger and bigger, and the 101 units of work will not feel any heavier than 100 units used to when you use 101 again.

In weight training the work load is progressively increased, so that once a muscle becomes used to a new stress level it is immediately hit with an even greater stress. So in our example above, you will place 102 units of stress on your thigh muscle as soon as it has become accustomed to handling 101 units. And by putting progressively more stress on a muscle it responds by continuing to grow larger and stronger.

To progressively increase the stress put on muscles when weight training, we increase both the weight used and the reps done with that weight. If you look at the workouts at the end of Chapter 3 you will see a range of repetitions listed for each exercise. We begin doing an exercise at the lower "guide number" for repetitions and slowly work up to the higher guide number. Then, when this is reached, we add five or ten pounds to the bar or machine being used and drop back to the lower guide number to begin working up again.

For back and leg exercises you should be able to add 10 pounds each time you drop back to the lower guide number for reps. And for the rest of the body you should be able to add five pounds each time.

TABLE 2-1 Progression on the Bench Press

	Monday	Wednesday	Friday
Week 1	40 × 8	40 × 9	40 × 10
Week 2	40 × 11	40 × 12	45 × 8
Week 3	45 × 9	45 × 11	45 × 12
Week 4	50 × 8	50 × 8	50 × 9

To fully clarify this concept of progression Table 2-1 is an example of how you might progress over a four-week period on the Bench Press. (Note that "40 × 10" means to do 10 repetitions with 40 pounds.)

When you do more than one set of movements you should reach the upper guide number of reps on all of the sets before increasing resistance. Table 2-2 is an example of this concept for a four-week period of doing Bent Rows.

TABLE 2-2 Progression on Bent Rows

Workout 1	Workout 2	Workout 3
50 × 8	50 × 10	50 × 11
50 × 8	50 × 9	50 × 10
50 × 8	50 × 8	50 × 10
Workout 4	**Workout 5**	**Workout 6**
50 × 12	50 × 12	50 × 12
50 × 11	50 × 12	50 × 12
50 × 10	50 × 11	50 × 12
Workout 7	**Workout 8**	**Workout 9**
60 × 10	60 × 12	60 × 12
60 × 9	60 × 10	60 × 11
60 × 8	60 × 10	60 × 11

HOW MUSCLES GROW

Bodybuilders used to think that weight workouts broke down muscle cells, which were then rebuilt to larger and stronger levels during periods of rest. Unfortunately, this notion of how muscles hypertrophy (grow in mass) is incorrect.

Physiologists have established that heavy exercise induces inhibition of catabolism in a muscle and that this catabolism-inhibition results in hypertrophy. To understand such a growth model, you must first know that within each muscle there is usually a balance between anabolism (a growth cycle of muscle tissue) and catabolism (a breaking-down cycle). When these cycles are balanced, there is no net change in muscle mass or strength. But if either anabolism can be increased or the catabolic rate decreased, a muscle will become larger and stronger.

One would think that exercise increases anabolism, when in reality it decreases catabolism which results in a net positive anabolic level. And *that* is how muscles grow!

BASIC DIET

Proper nutrition is a key ingredient in any health and fitness success formula. As much as faulty nutrition is the quickest way to ruin your body, good nutritional practices are the best way to promote buoyantly good health. And hand in hand with weight training, good diet can turn you into a superwoman!

To give you a full understanding of good nutrition, we would need to devote this whole book just to that subject. Since this is impractical, we suggest that you read as many books and articles on the subject as possible, which will help you to formulate your own individualized nutritional program. And until you do so, you can use the following general rules of healthy eating:

1. Be sure that all of your foods are as fresh (as close to nature) as possible. Avoid processed, refined, canned, frozen, and packaged foods, all of which have much of their nutritional value removed and have excessive amounts of sugar and chemical preservatives added.

2. Limit the amount of fat (particularly animal fat) in your diet. Don't fry foods. A gram of fat yields nine calories of energy when it is metabolized, while both protein and carbohydrate yield only four calories per gram. So it's logical that the bulk of your diet should consist of protein and carbohydrate if you are trying to limit the number of calories in your diet.

3. Restrict the use of grains and milk products in your diet. Both of these food groups are highly allergenic to most people, and allergenic foods retain large quantities of water in the body, which tends to give you a "puffy" look.

4. Use food supplements, but use them conservatively. Take small amounts (the dosages recommended on each bottle of vitamins) of A, B, and C vitamins to start. Then as you become more knowledgeable about food supplementation, you can slowly add other vitamins and minerals.

5. Eat one-half to one gram of protein per pound of body weight. Don't overload your diet with protein, however, because it will cause a strain on your kidneys.

6. Eat only natural (complex) carbohydrates for your sugar sources, and avoid all processed (simple) carbohydrates. So for energy instead of eating a pastry loaded with refined sugar and flour, eat a piece or two of fruit, a bowl of whole-grain cereal, or a plate of brown rice.

7. If you are overweight, reduce your daily caloric intake by 10 to 20 percent until such time as your body fat level is normalized. To do this most easily, simply cut back on the amount of fat in your diet, and avoid all refined carbohydrates.

8. Eat at least two servings of high-roughage food per day. Bran cereal, pears, salad greens, and whole-grain bread are good sources of roughage.

9. Drink plenty of liquids every day, particularly six to ten glasses of fresh, pure water daily.

10. Eat as wide a variety of foods each week as possible.

Following these guidelines, here is a sample weight-reduction diet for a single day. (The size of each portion of food will vary with the size and caloric requirements of each individual.)

Breakfast—sunflower seeds, two pears, bran cereal with a minimum of nonfat, raw milk supplements.

Snack—fruit and/or nuts.

Lunch—broiled fish, baked potato (dry, no butter!), large salad with lemon and vinegar, iced tea with honey or Sweet 'n Low, supplements.

Snack—scoop of tuna salad with a minimum of dressing.

Dinner—baked chicken, brown rice, green beans or peas, fruit, water, supplements.

Try this diet for a few weeks, and you'll notice the fat rapidly melting away. And if you're *not* losing fat fast enough, simply reduce the size of the portions of food you eat.

SLEEP AND REST

In order for muscles to grow larger and stronger at an optimum rate, they have to fully recuperate between workouts. And this recuperation can only take place if your body is given sufficient rest and sleep.

Your energy balances are like your checking account. You write checks (use up energy) when you take a workout, have a sleepless night, eat poorly, or worry too much. And you make deposits by sleeping, resting, keeping a tranquil mind, and maintaining a healthy diet.

To encourage muscle growth, you must keep your energy balance positive, the same as you must keep your checking account in the black to please your bank. The best way to keep in the black with your energy cycles is to get enough sleep and rest.

This picture, and the one that follows on the next page, illustrate the kind of clothing that can be worn during workouts.

Always **use a spotter (training partner) when training with heavy weights or when training to exhaustion on a certain exercise.**

Unfortunately, it's very difficult to tell you how much sleep to get, because human sleep needs vary so greatly. One woman might get along fine on four hours of sleep per night, while another may need 10 hours just to appear halfway normal each day.

You *should* try to get eight hours of sleep each night, plus perhaps a 30-minute nap during the day. And you should also avoid being too hyperactive during the day. If you feel tired or sleepy all day, you need more sleep and rest. But if you have trouble falling asleep at night, you are probably getting too much sleep.

WHAT TO WEAR

Any type of athletic clothing is suitable for weight training. Women most commonly wear shorts and a T-shirt or a leotard and tights. You should also wear shoes, and in cold weather a full warm-up suit is advisable.

The real key in choosing what to wear for a workout is to find clothing that doesn't bind your joints. Weight training requires moving your limbs over their full range of movement, and tight-fitting clothing restricts such movement.

BREAK-IN AND MUSCLE SORENESS

Since weight training is much heavier work than you've ever done before, your muscles can become very sore if you try to jump into doing a full program your very first workout. Therefore, you should break in slowly and carefully.

Start your break-in by doing only one set of each exercise for the first week, even though multiple sets are listed for most of the exercises. In the second week do two sets of each exercise where two or more sets are recommended. Finally, in the third week you can begin doing the complete workout.

Be careful about adding weight to your barbell or machine before the fourth week of training. During the first two or three weeks you should use only the recommended starting poundages, adding weight only when your body has become fully accustomed to the heavier work load.

An inevitable consequence of applying a much-heavier-than-usual load to a muscle is stiffness and soreness. The muscle just isn't used to heavy stress, and nature responds by making it sore. This soreness can be avoided, or at least reduced in severity, in several ways:

1. Hot baths and hot showers will increase blood circulation and relax the muscles.

2. Massage will alleviate soreness, but sometimes the pain of manipulating sore muscles can be worse than the original pain.

3. Repeating the previous day's workout usually will hurt a little, but it will cut the overall pain considerably.

4. Break in slowly when you begin to train. Use light weights and only one to two sets per exercise until your body grows accustomed to the stress.

EXERCISE FORM

In order to isolate resistance on the muscles being trained it's essential that you eliminate extraneous body movement from each exercise. By kicking your legs or bending your back, it will be much easier to get a weight up on each repetition. But such practices (known in weight training circles as *cheating*) actually rob you of much of the benefit of an exercise.

It's also essential to move the weight every repetition over the full range of motion that each joint permits. This essentially involves moving the weight so each muscle is taken from full extension to full contraction and then back again to full extension. Short-range movements can be harmful to the muscles, and can reduce body flexibility. Full-range movements, on the contrary, actually promote flexibility.

WARM-UPS

Weight training is heavier and more stressful exercise than anything you've ever done, and without a proper warm-up it is possible to sustain an injury. But with a good warm-up and a steady training pace, you should have no problems whatsoever with injuries.

Scientific studies have shown that you will actually get a better workout if you warm up your body before weight training. This is because the warm-up makes your muscles and connective tissues more supple, plus it makes neuromuscular coordination more precise.

Spend five to ten minutes warming up. Start with three to five minutes of jogging or jumping rope. Then spend the rest of your time doing light calisthenics and stretching movements. Then once your pulse rate has been accelerated and you've broken into a sweat, you'll be ready to move on to your weight workout.

SAFETY

There are two primary safety procedures that should be followed during every weight-training session. The first of these is to *always* use collars on the outside of a barbell. It's undoubtedly easier to leave the collars off, but this allows plates to slide off the low end of a barbell whenever the arms are extended unevenly in an exercise. And once the plates slide off one side, the weighted side will whip viciously downward, putting sufficient torque on the barbell to injure your lower back or some other joint.

The second safety rule you should follow is to always use a spotter when training with heavy weights on the Bench Press, Squat, and other exercises in which you can be pinned under the bar if you fail to complete a repetition of the movement. This way, your spotter can rescue you whenever you are pinned under the bar.

BREATHING

We have probably heard more questions about how to breathe while lifting weights than about any other weight-training technique. Every woman with whom we have talked has been confused at some time about how to breathe while exercising.

There are essentially three methods of breathing, each of which has an army of adherents. They are as follows:

1. Breathe in during the exertion phase and out during the relaxation phase.

2. Breathe in during the relaxation phase of a movement and out during the exertion phase.

3. Breathe naturally. There are naturally occurring points in each exercise at which you will breathe in and out without even thinking about it. And if you are taking in enough air to keep from passing out, you're breathing just fine.

We endorse the third of these alternatives.

ONWARD

In Chapter 3 we will give you a basic pool of 18 exercises and several graduated beginning-level workouts. This will get you started correctly in weight training.

3

Beginning Exercises and Workouts

In this chapter we will start you shaping and toning your body with weight training by presenting a pool of 18 basic exercises, then a series of progressively more difficult training routines. The exercises illustrated and explained here include movements using free weights (barbells and dumbbells), Universal Gym machines, and Nautilus machines.

You will use the basic group of exercises—adding more as you gain experience as a bodybuilder—for as long as you train with weights, so be scrupulously careful to learn correct exercise form from the very start. Bad habits learned now will be almost impossible to break a year from now, and faulty exercise form can lead to muscle and/or joint injuries.

For each exercise in this chapter there will be a detailed written description of the movement, plus clear photos of the correct form for the exercise. Study both carefully before attempting the movement, and check your exercise form in a mirror as you work out. And, if you have any doubts about how to correctly perform an exercise, consult a knowledgeable friend or gym instructor. It would be better to pay for instruction than to learn poor exercise form. But by carefully analyzing the description and photos of each exercise in this book, you will have no difficulty in learning correct form.

Near the end of this chapter, you will find a number of suggested weight-training programs, each graduated in difficulty from the lowest beginning level to an intermediate level corresponding to four to six months of training experience. These programs will be specifically aimed at slimming, weight gaining, sports performance improvement, appearance or body contours improvement, and health and fitness improvement. And there will be suggested workouts for use with free weights, Universal Gyms, and Nautilus machines. All you need to do is pick the workouts appropriate to your level of experience, goals, and the type of equipment that is available to you.

POOL OF BEGINNERS' EXERCISES

Sit-ups

1. Emphasis—Sit-ups directly stress all of the muscles of your abdomen. Particular stress is placed on the upper half of the frontal abdominal muscle group.

2. Starting Position—Lie on your back on the floor, or lie on an abdominal board. Hook your feet under a heavy piece of furniture or under the strap or rollers of the abdominal board. Bend your knees at about a 45-degree angle to relieve strain on your lower back as you do the movement. Place your hands behind your neck.

3. The Movement—Slowly curl your torso up off the floor until your upper body makes a right angle with your legs. As you curl up, your shoulders should leave the floor first, then the middle of your back, and finally the small of your back. Return slowly to the starting position and repeat.

4. Training Tips—You can cross your arms on your chest as an alternative to placing them behind your neck. Regardless of the arm position, however, be very sure not to jerk your body up when doing a sit-up. The key is to do the movement slowly and under full control, which activates the maximum number of muscle cells in your abdominal muscles.

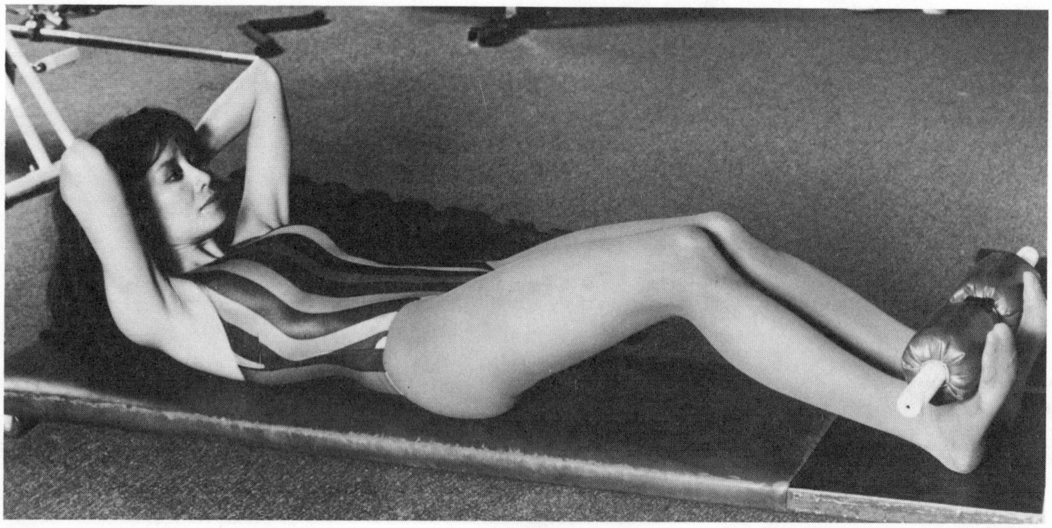

Sit-ups—start.

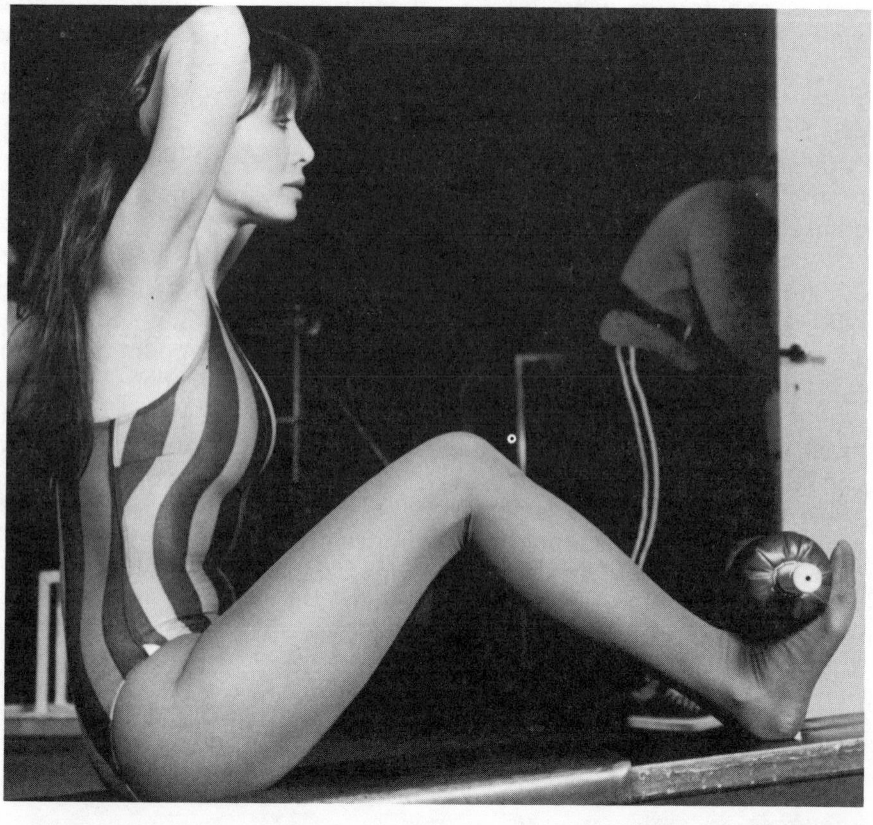

Sit-ups—finish.

Standing Calf Raise/Standing Calf Machine Toe Raise

1. Emphasis—This movement stresses the gastrocnemius and soleus muscles at the back of your lower legs.

2. Starting Position—Place a barbell across your shoulders and behind you neck, balancing it in position with your hands. Stand with your toes and the balls of your feet on a 4 × 4-inch or a 2 × 4-inch block of wood. Your feet should be about eight to ten inches apart, your toes pointed straight ahead. Standing erect, relax your calf muscles and stretch them by allowing your heels to travel below the level of your toes. The lower you can get your heels at the beginning of this movement, the better.

3. The Movement—Keeping your legs straight, rise up as high as possible on your toes. Lower your heels slowly back to the starting position, and repeat for the required number of repetitions.

Standing Calf Raise—finish.

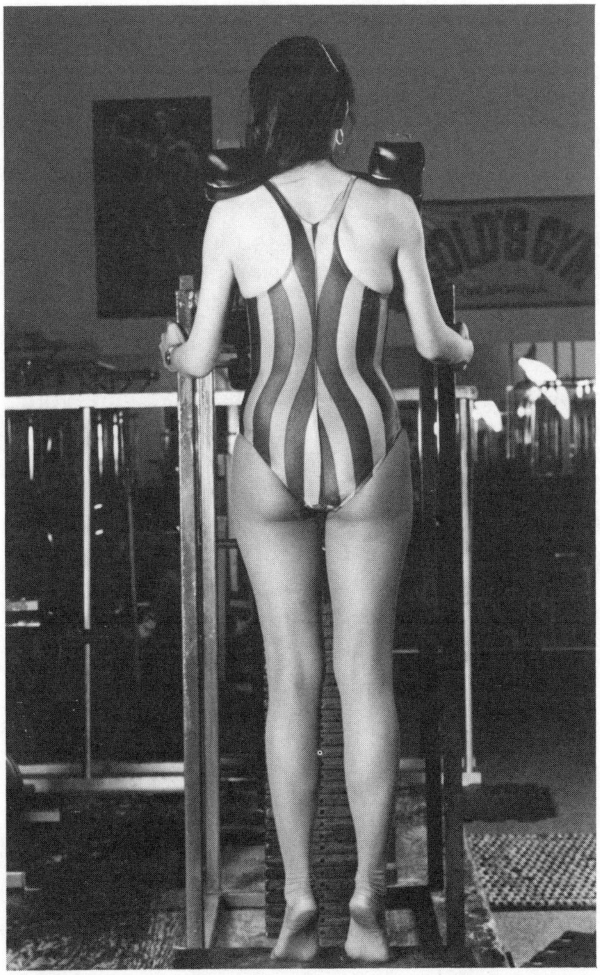

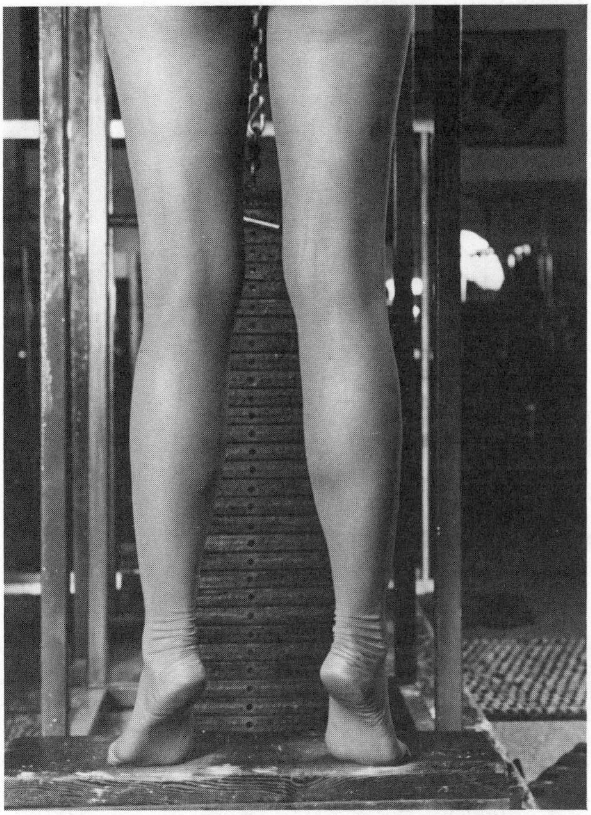

Standing Calf Raise—finish with toes out.

Standing Calf Raise—finish with toes in.

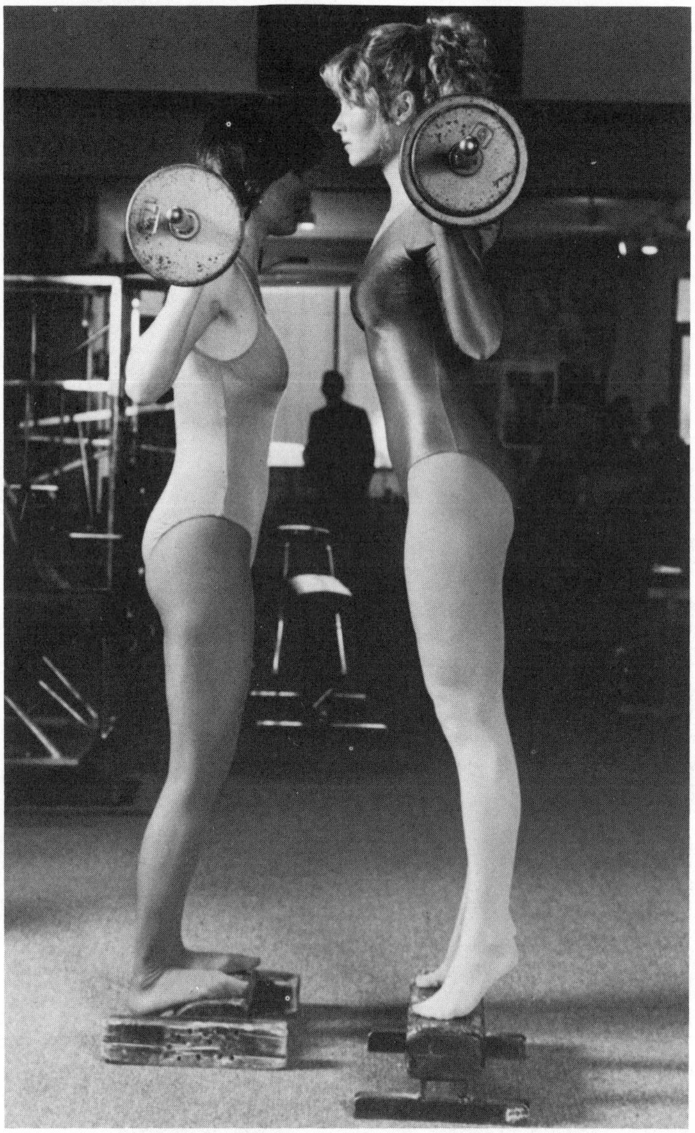

Standing Calf Raise using barbell.

4. Training Tips—You'll find it somewhat difficult to balance your body with a barbell behind your neck and your toes up on a block of wood, but if you rise up on your toes slowly, you should be able to manage it with reasonable stability. In well-organized gyms, there is invariably a special calf machine that eliminates this problem. Such a machine consists of a yoke that passes over the shoulders. There are several ways that the weight is attached to such a yoke, but all of them allow you to place direct resistance on your calf muscles without encountering the balance problem.

Once you have completed your first set of Toe Raises with your feet pointed straight ahead, do your second set with your feet pointed outward at a 45-degree angle. On your third set, point them inward at a 45-degree angle. These varying foot positions (pointed outward, straight ahead, and inward) should be used on all calf exercises, since each foot position stresses the calves in a slightly different way from the others. The combination of all three foot positions in your workouts will give you superior muscle tone and strength in your calves.

Leg Press Machine Toe Press

1. Emphasis—Like the Standing Calf Raise, this exercise stresses the gastrocnemius and soleus muscles at the back of your lower legs.

2. Starting Position—This starting position for Toe Presses on a Leg Press machine is fundamentally the same for Universal, Nautilus, and free-weight Leg Press machines. Place only the toes and balls of your feet on the pedals or foot board and straighten your legs. Relax your calf muscles and stretch them by allowing your heels to travel as far away from you and past your toes as possible.

3. The Movement—Keeping your legs straight throughout the movement, simply extend your toes as far away from your body as possible. Return slowly back to the starting point, and repeat for the required number of repetitions.

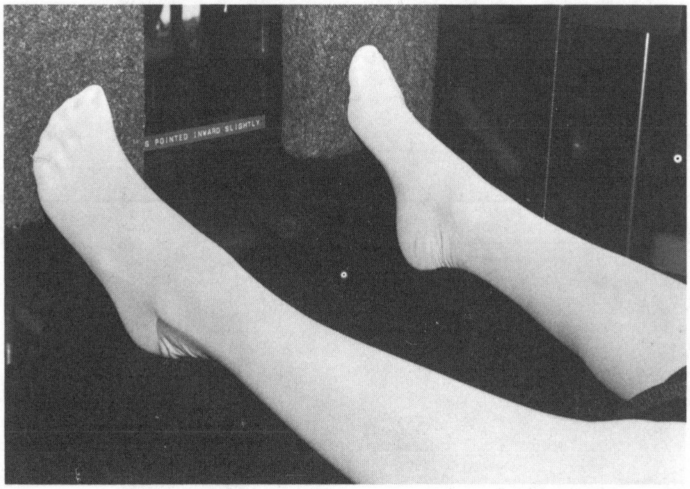

Calf stretching movement demonstrated on Leg Press Nautilus machine.

4. Training Tips—As with the Standing Calf Raise, switch regularly between the three toe positions previously discussed. You can also experiment on all calf exercises with different foot-stance widths. Sometimes merely moving the feet an inch closer together or an inch farther apart will completely change the effect of an exercise on the calf muscles.

Squat

1. Emphasis—This exercise is one of the best movements you can do, because it affects most of the body's major muscle groups and stimulates the body's metabolism. The Squat works primarily the frontal thigh muscles, the hips and buttocks, the hamstrings at the back of the upper legs, and the lower back. The abdomen, upper back, calves, and shoulders are stimulated secondarily.

2. Starting Position—Stand erect with a barbell behind your neck, as in the starting position for the Standing Calf Raise. Place your heels about 10 to 12 inches apart, with your toes angled out about 45-degrees on each side. Tighten your back muscles, which will allow you to keep your torso upright during the movement.

3. The Movement—Fix your eyes on a point about shoulder high and keep them there through the movement. Then slowly bend your knees, and lower your body into a fully squatting position. Be sure to keep your torso upright and your head up during the whole movement. Once your upper thigh bones have gone below an imaginary line parallel to the floor, slowly return to the starting position by straightening your legs. As you squat down, it's important that your knees travel directly outward over your ankles, i.e., out at 45-degree angles to each side. Repeat the Squat movement for the required number of repetitions.

4. Training Tip—If you lack ankle flexibility, you'll find it difficult to balance yourself while squatting. In such cases, you can make your balance more secure by resting your heels on a 2 × 4-inch board during the movement.

Use 2 × 4-inch board to keep your balance during Squats.

Leg Press

1. Emphasis—This movement strongly stresses the frontal thigh muscles, hips, and buttocks. It places secondary emphasis on the hamstring muscles at the backs of the thighs, on the calves, and on the lower back.

2. Starting Position—The starting position for Leg Presses on Universal and Nautilus machines is fundamentally the same. Simply sit erect in the respective machine's seat, grasp the handles provided at the sides of the seat, and place your feet flat on the pedals in front of you. On the vertical free-weight Leg Press machine, lie on your back with your hips directly below the weight platform, place your feet at shoulder width on the platform, straighten your legs, and release the weight stops on both sides of the machine.

Leg Press on vertical free-weight machine—start.

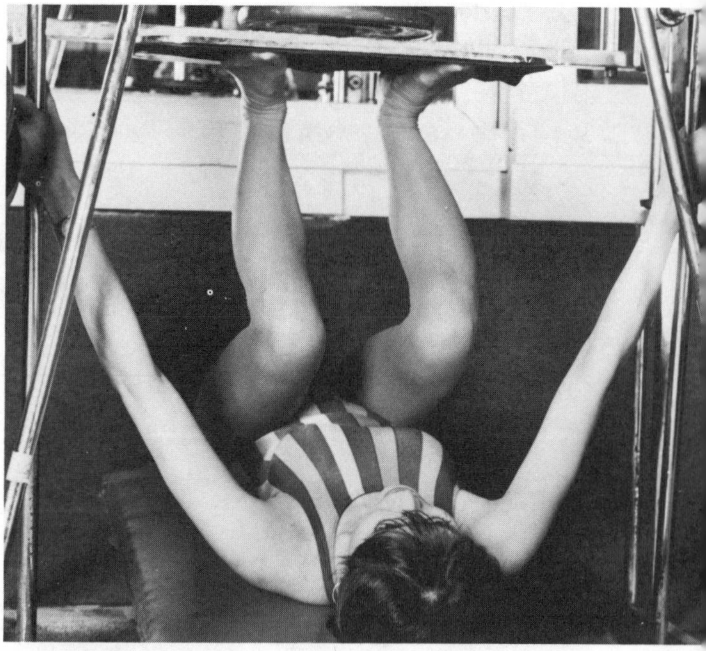

Leg Press on vertical free-weight machine—finish.

3. The Movement—Regardless of the type of Leg Press machine used, simply bend and straighten your legs over their full range of motion for the required number of repetitions.

4. Training Tips—On the Universal and Nautilus machines, you can increase the range of motion for Leg Presses by simply adjusting the movable seat forward toward the pedals. On the Universal machine, it is essential to keep your back straight and your head up throughout the movement. Hunching your shoulders and thrusting your head forward can leave you open to back injuries.

Bent Rowing

1. Emphasis—This movement stresses the large latissimus dorsi muscles of your upper back, with secondary stress placed on the trapezius, erector spinae, biceps, and forearms.

2. Starting Position—With your feet set shoulder width apart, bend over at the waist until your torso is parallel to the floor. Unlock your knees slightly, and keep them bent throughout the movement. Grasp a barbell with a shoulder-width grip, your palms facing your shins. Your arms should be straight and hanging straight down from your torso at the beginning of the movement, and the barbell should be off the floor.

3. The Movement—Making sure that your upper arms travel out to the sides, bend your arms and pull the barbell straight upward until it touches the lower edge of your rib cage. Lower the bar back to the starting position, and repeat for the required number of reps.

4. Training Tips—On most barbell exercises, and particularly on the Bent Rowing movement, you should periodically vary the width of your grip. Varying grip widths will put differing degrees of stress on the muscles you are working. The greater the number of grips you can use, the greater the development you can expect from a particular movement.

Barbell Bent Rowing. Tip: Vary the width of your grip.

Lat Pulldown

1. Emphasis—Like the Bent Rowing movement, Lat Pulldowns primarily stress the large latissimus dorsi muscles of the upper back. Secondary emphasis is placed on the biceps, forearms, and trapezius.

2. Starting Position—In a Nautilus torso-arm machine fasten the lap belt to restrain your body in the machine, and grasp the lat bar handles with your palms facing inward. Using a Universal Gym or free-standing lat machine grasp the lat bar with your palms facing forward and your hands set three to six inches wider than your shoulders on each side. If you are on a Universal Gym machine—as well as on some free-standing lat machines—either sit or kneel directly below the pulley. On most newer-model lat machines there will be a seat to sit on and a horizontal bar under which you can wedge your knees to restrain your body as you do the movement. On all three variations of the Lat Pulldown, your arms should be perfectly straight at the start of the movement.

3. The Movement—Slowly bend your arms and pull the lat bar down until it touches at the base of your neck, either in front of or behind your head. Return to the starting point, and repeat for the required number of repetitions.

4. Training Tips—You can pull the bar down behind your neck for a full set, to the front of your neck for a full set, or do your set alternating a rep behind your neck with one in front of your neck. Pulling the bar down behind your neck emphasizes the upper section of the latissimus dorsi, while pulling it to the front of your neck puts greater stress on the lower lats.

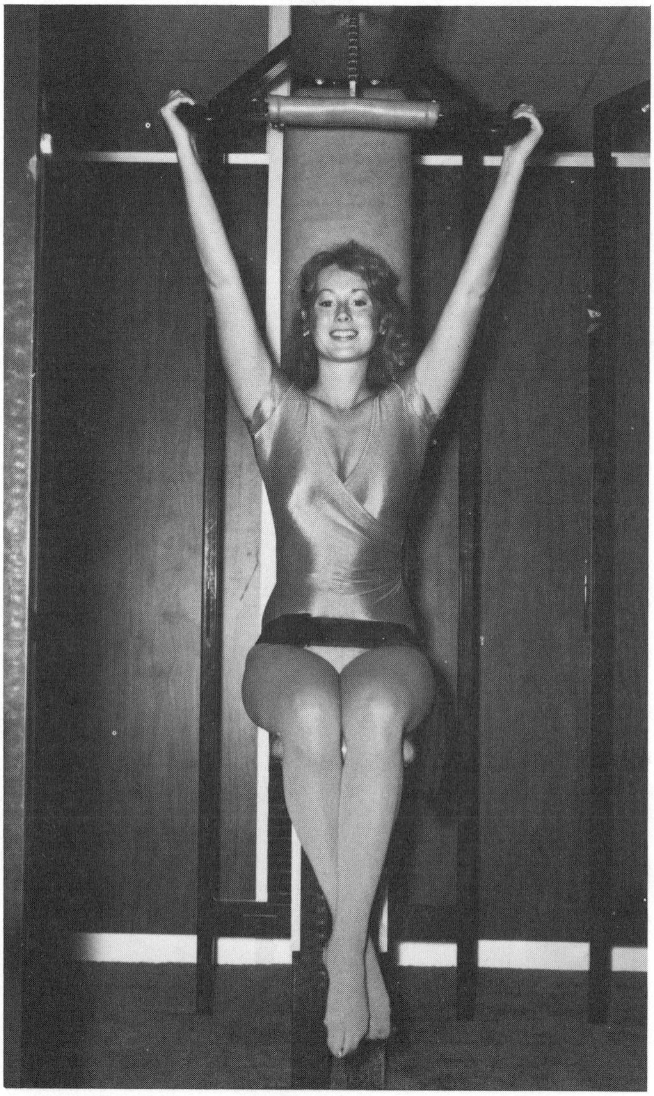

Lat Pulldown on Nautilus machine—start.

Lat Pulldown on free-weight machine—behind the neck.

Lat Pulldown on free-weight machine—in front of neck.

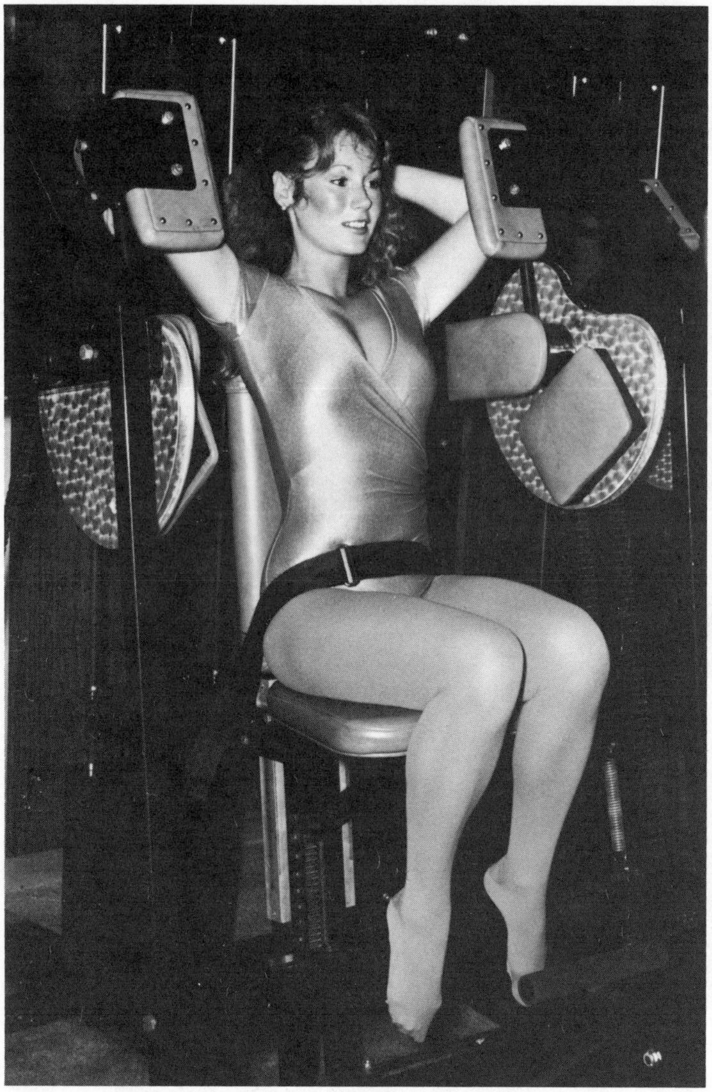

Nautilus Pullover—start. Be sure to strap in belt to restrain your body.

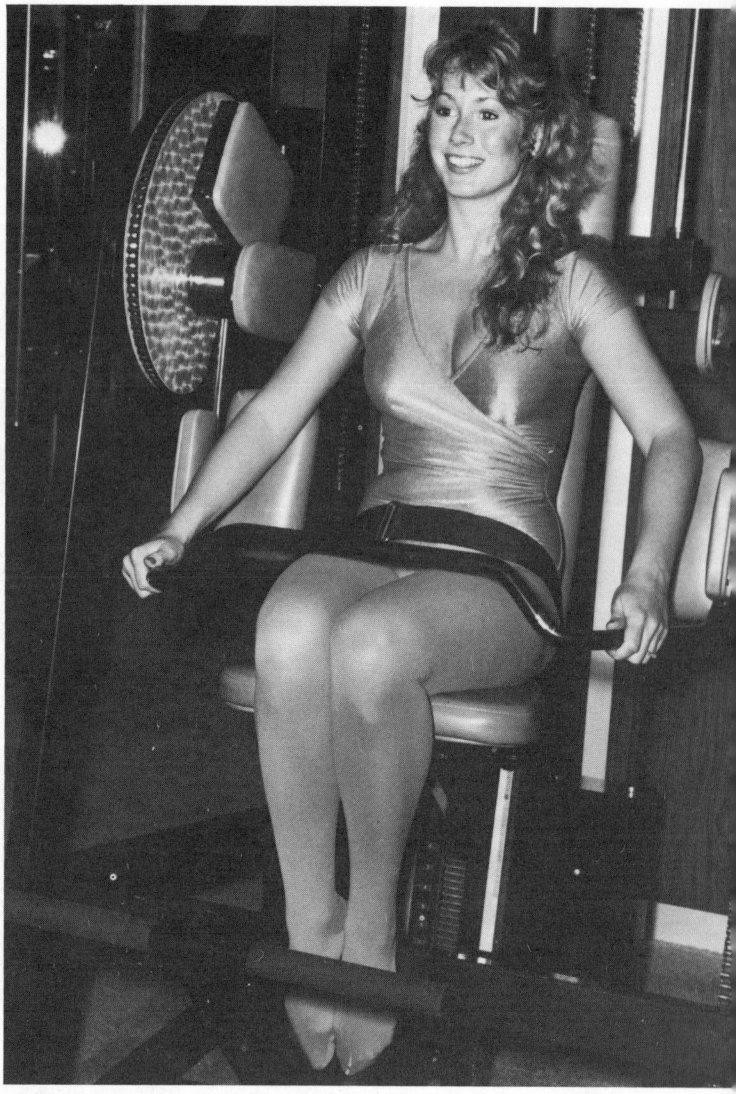

Nautilus Pullover—finish.

Nautilus Pullovers

1. **Emphasis**—Major stress in this exercise is placed on the latissimus dorsi muscles. Secondary emphasis is placed on the pectorals, abdominals, deltoids, and triceps.

2. **Starting Position**—Adjust the seat upward or downward so that your shoulder joints are at the same level as the pivot point of the Nautilus cam (pulley) on each side of the machine. Fasten the lap belt across your hips to restrain your body during the movement. Push down on the foot pedal until the pads of the machine's movement arm are forward enough so you can comfortably place your elbows on the pads. Grasp the bar connecting the pads. Slowly release leg pressure on the foot pedal and allow your elbows to move backward in semicircles as far as possible.

3. **The Movement**—Move your elbows in semicircles forward and downward until the movement arm crossbar touches your thighs. Pause in this position for a slow count of two. Return to the starting position and repeat for the required number of repetitions.

4. **Training Tip**—When exiting from the machine, push down again on the foot pedal to take weight off your elbows. Remove your elbows from the pads and release leg pressure from the foot pedal. Unbuckle the lap belt and exit from the machine.

Bench Press

1. Emphasis—Bench Presses stress the pectorals, deltoids, and triceps of the upper body. In fact, Bench Presses are one of the best upper body exercises in existence.

2. Starting Position—Lying on your back, take a shoulder-width grip on a barbell, your palms toward your feet. Your arms should be straight and the barbell supported directly above your chest. On a Universal Gym lie on your back on the bench so your shoulder joints are directly under the Bench Press handles. Grasp the handles with your palms facing your feet and straighten your arms. In the Nautilus double chest machine sit in the seat and buckle the seat belt over your hips. Push with your feet on the foot pedal until the Bench Press handles are in a position where you can grasp them with your palms facing inward. Push even harder on the pedal and straighten your arms.

Bench Press using barbell—start.

Bench Press using barbell—finish. Be sure to use a spotter (partner) when training to fatigue.

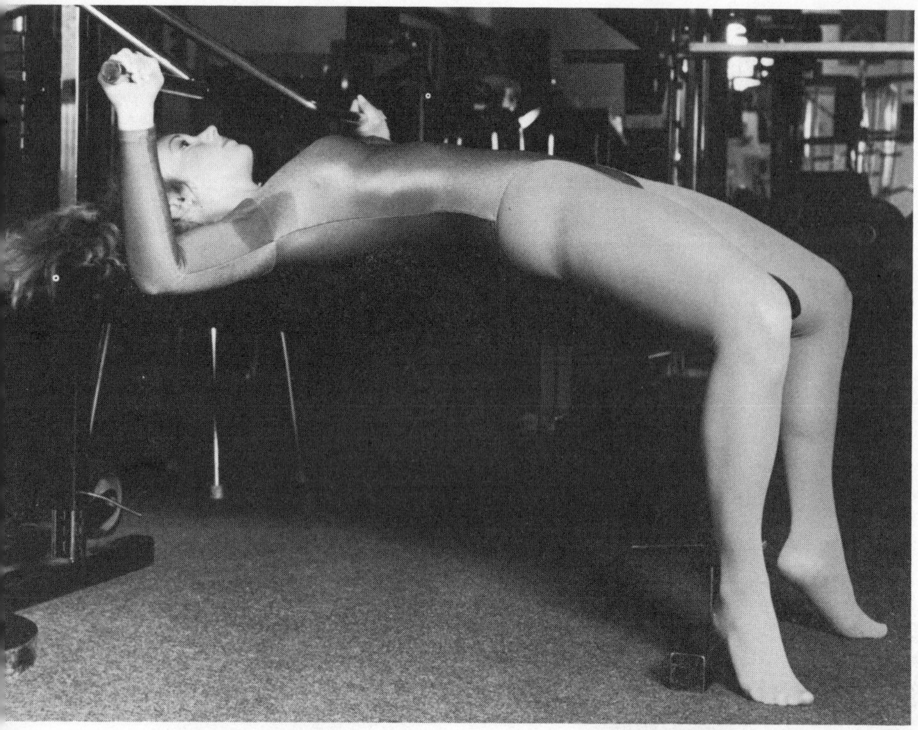

Bench Press on Universal Gym machine—midpoint.

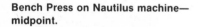

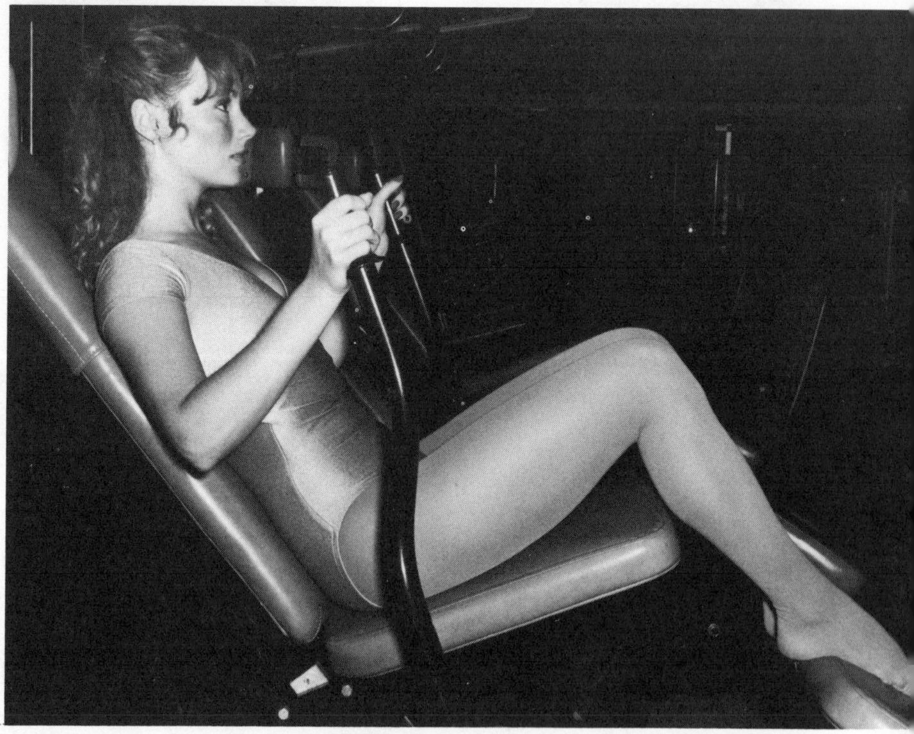

Bench Press on Nautilus machine—midpoint.

3. The Movement—Making sure that your upper arms travel directly out to the sides, slowly bend your arms and lower the weight straight downward until it touches your chest or, on the Nautilus machine, until you have lowered your hands as far as possible. Push back up to the starting position, and repeat for the required number of repetitions.

4. Training Tip—Be sure not to arch your back up to complete a repetition. This takes stress off the muscles being worked, defeating the purpose of doing the movement in the first place.

Military Press

1. Emphasis—Military Presses stress primarily the deltoids and triceps, with secondary emphasis placed on the upper pectorals, trapezius, and back.

2. Starting Position—Pull a barbell up to your shoulders with a shoulder-width grip, your palms facing away from your body when the weight is at your shoulders. Stand erect and maintain this position throughout the entire movement.

3. The Movement—Slowly push the barbell straight up past your face until your arms are locked out straight and the barbell is directly over the top of your head. Slowly lower the weight back to the starting position, and repeat for the required number of repetitions.

4. Training Tip—Be very careful not to bend backward as you press the weight up. This will make the movement easier to complete but will rob your shoulders and triceps of part of the stress they should be receiving.

Military Press—finish and start. Be very careful not to bend backward.

Seated Press

1. Emphasis—This exercise stresses primarily the deltoids and triceps, with secondary emphasis placed on the upper pectorals, trapezius, and back.

2. Starting Position—On the Nautilus double shoulder machine, adjust the seat so your shoulders are level with the handles of the overhead pressing apparatus. Grasp the handles with your palms facing inward. On a Universal Gym face the machine and sit on the stool with your shoulders directly under the pressing handles. Grasp the handles of the movement arm so that your palms are facing forward. With a barbell start in the same position as for a Military Press, except that you will be sitting at the end of a flat exercise bench instead of standing erect.

3. The Movement—Slowly push the weight straight upward until your arms are locked out straight and the weight is directly overhead. Slowly lower the weight back to the starting position, and repeat for the required number of repetitions.

4. Training Tip—Invariably, you will find that you will not be able to use as much weight in a Barbell Seated Press as in a Military Press, since doing any exercise in a seated position isolates your legs from the movement.

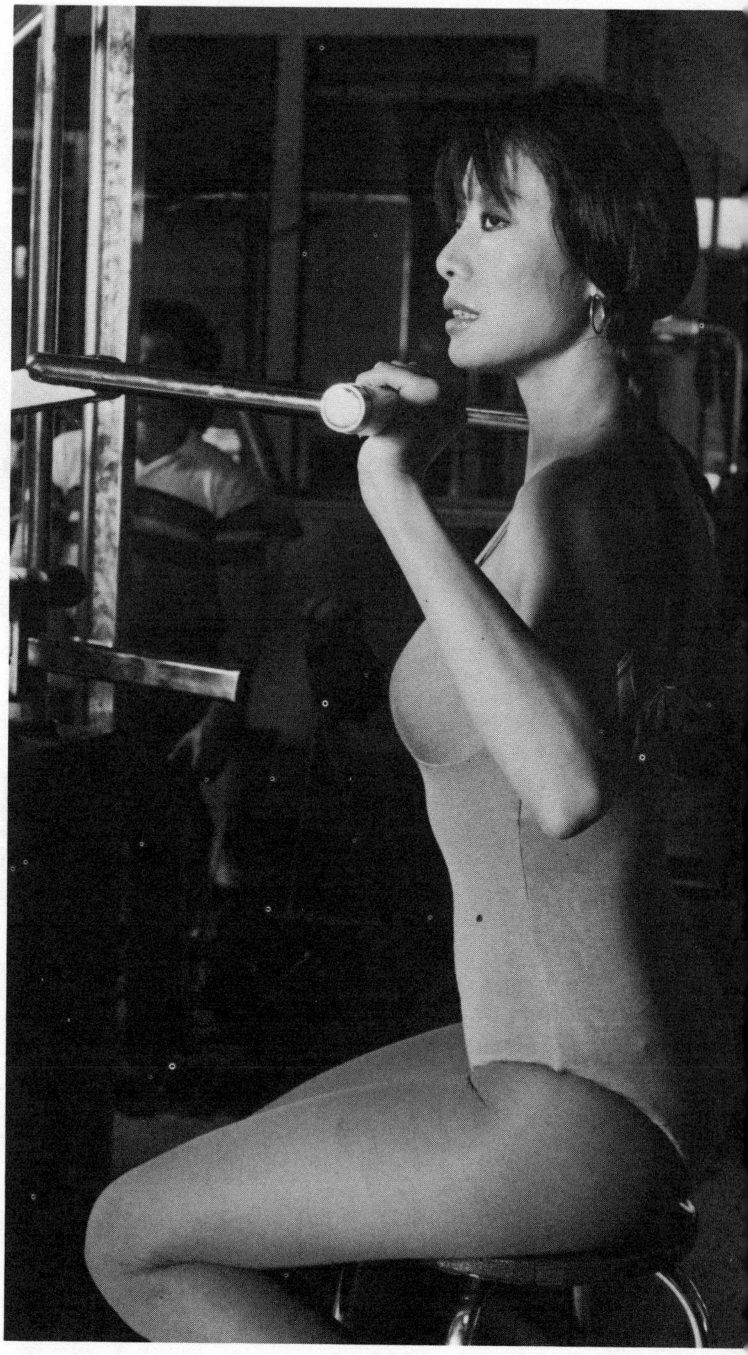

Seated Press on Universal Gym machine—start. Finish by slowly pushing weight upward until your arms are straight and elbows locked out.

Seated Press on Universal Gym machine, facing away—start. Finish by raising arms until locked straight up.

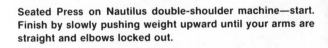

Seated Press on Nautilus double-shoulder machine—start. Finish by slowly pushing weight upward until your arms are straight and elbows locked out.

Barbell Curl

1. Emphasis—This movement places primary stress on the biceps and secondary stress on the muscles of your forearms.

2. Starting Position—Stand erect with a shoulder-width grip on a barbell, your palms facing away from your body. Your upper arms should be pinned to the sides of your torso and the barbell resting across your upper thighs. At the start of the movement, your arms should be straight.

3. The Movement—Moving just your forearms, bend your arms and move the barbell in a semicircle from your thighs to your chin. Slowly lower the weight along the same arc back to the starting position, and repeat for the required number of repetitions.

4. Training Tip—Be sure to keep your upper body motionless as you curl the weight up and down. Moving your torso and bending your back to get the barbell up to the finish position is cheating and will rob the movement of much of its effectiveness.

Barbell Curl—finish and start.

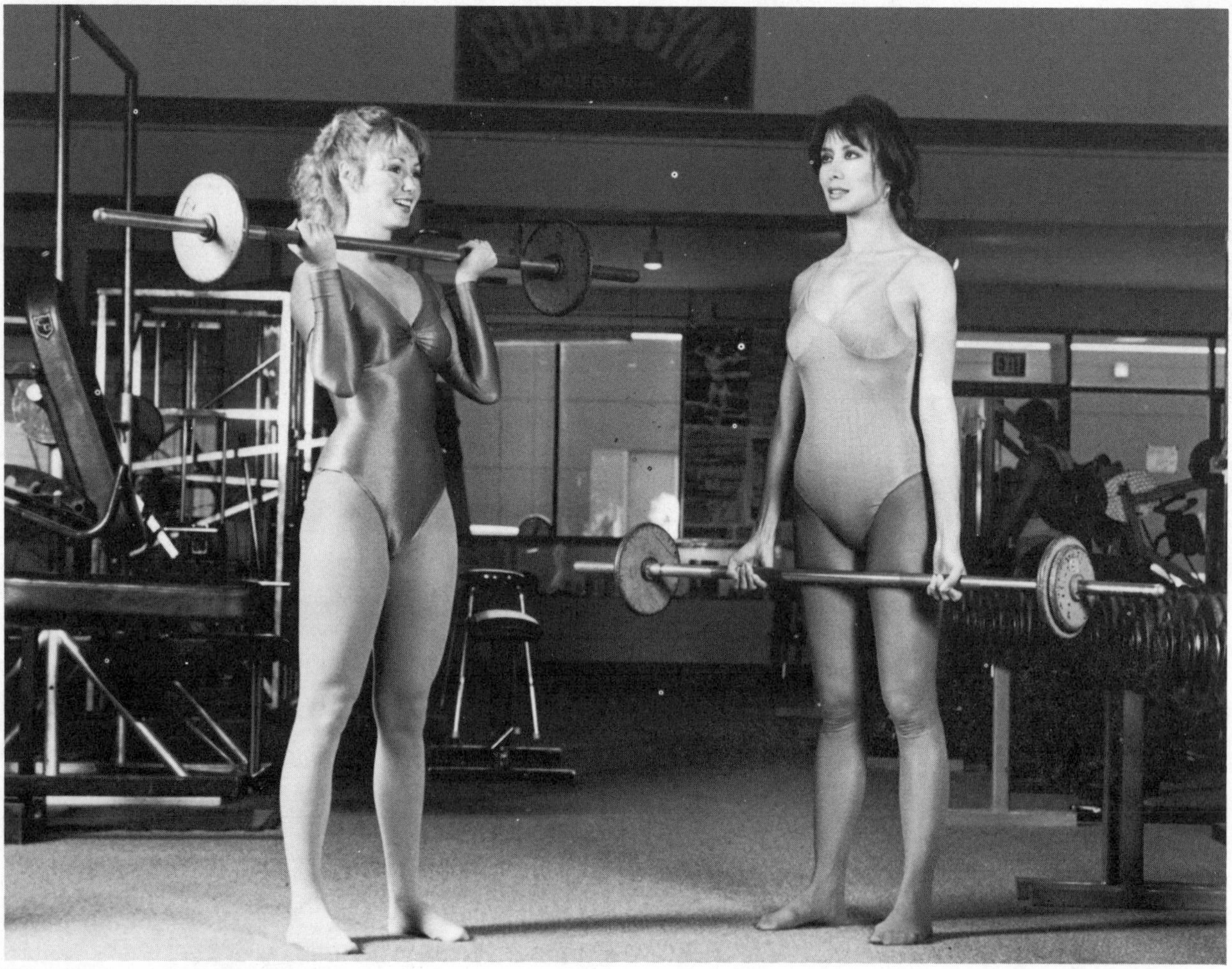

Pulley Curl—start.

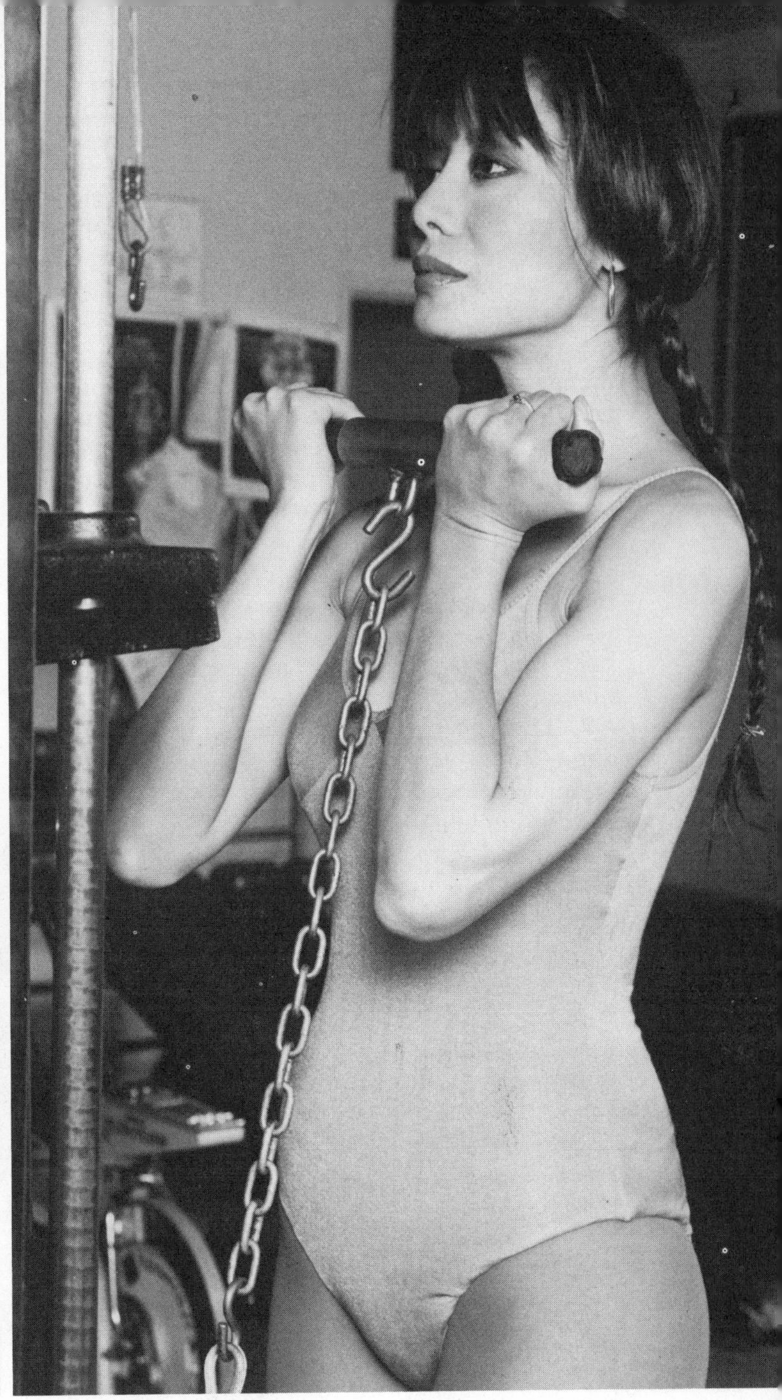
Pulley Curl—finish.

Pulley Curl

1. Emphasis—As with the Barbell Curl, this exercise places primary stress on the biceps and secondary stress on the muscles of the forearms.

2. Starting Position—Grasp the handle of a Universal Gym floor pulley with a relatively narrow grip (eight to twelve inches between your index fingers), your palms facing away from your body. Place your feet six to eight inches back from the pulley and stand erect. Pin your upper arms to the sides of your torso.

3. The Movement—Moving just your forearms, bend your elbows and move the pulley handle in a semicircle from your thighs to your chin. Slowly lower the weight along the same arc back to the starting position. Repeat for the required number of repetitions.

4. Training Tip—This exercise can also be done lying on your back on the floor, with your feet facing the pulley. In this variation of Pulley Curls, you will find that you can use much less weight than when standing because the floor completely restricts your upper arms from moving.

Nautilus Curl

1. Emphasis—This movement places strong emphasis on the biceps muscles and lesser emphasis on the muscles of the forearms.

2. Starting Position—Adjust the seat on a Nautilus multi-biceps machine so you can sit in the machine with your shoulders two to three inches lower than the angled pad in front of your neck. Place your elbows on the pad and grasp the handles of the machine. You will need to come up out of your seat a few inches to do this comfortably. Sit back down and fully straighten your arms.

3. The Movement—Slowly curl both handles of the machine to the full range of motion of your biceps. Pause momentarily, lower slowly back to the starting point, and repeat for the required number of repetitions.

4. Training Tip—You can curl your arms alternately for a variation on this basic movement. Simply curl both arms fully; then lower one hand completely and curl it back up. Lower the other hand completely and curl it back up. Repeat alternately in this fashion until your biceps are fully fatigued.

Nautilus Curl—finish, curling both arms.

Nautilus Curl—finish, curling right arm.

Nautilus Curl—start.

Nautilus Curl—finish, curling left arm.

Pulley Pushdown

1. Emphasis—This exercise places considerable stress on the triceps muscles on the back of your upper arm and lesser stress on the forearm muscles.

2. Starting Position—Stand six inches back from the lat pulley of a Universal Gym or the lat pulley on a free-standing pulley apparatus. Grasp the pulley handle with a narrow grip (two to four inches between your index fingers) and your palms facing away from your body. Straighten your arms fully, so the pulley handle rests across your upper thighs. Press your upper arms against the sides of your torso, and keep them in this position throughout the movement.

3. The Movement—From this basic starting position, slowly bend your arms and allow the pulley handle to travel in a semicircle from your thighs to your chin. Return the handle back along the same arc to the starting position, and repeat for the required number of repetitions.

4. Training Tips—This movement can be done with a reversed grip, or with one arm at a time, for variety. On all variations of Pulley Pushdowns, it is essential to restrict all back-and-forth movements of your torso while doing the exercise. Such *loose* exercise form robs the movement of much of its effectiveness.

Pulley Pushdown—start.

Pulley Pushdown—finish.

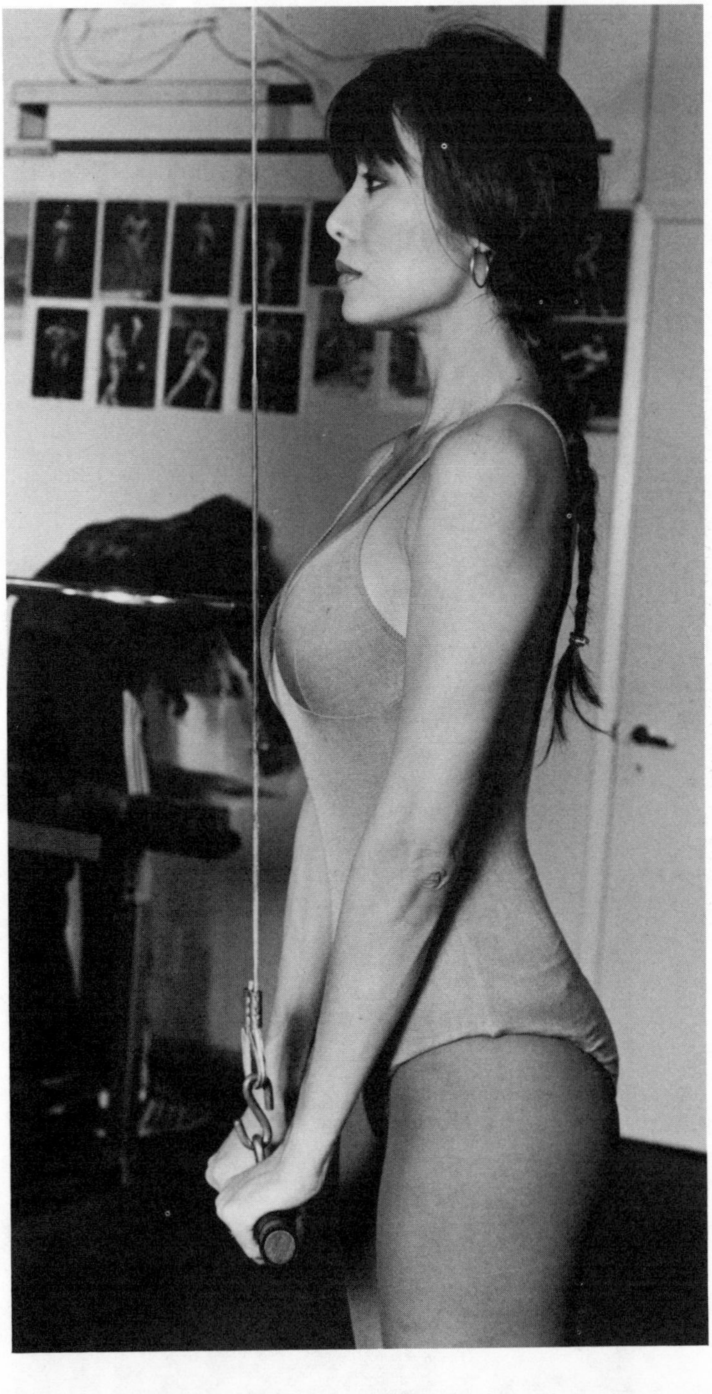

Lying Triceps Extension

1. Emphasis—This movement places great stress on the triceps muscles at the back of your upper arms.

2. Starting Position—Adopt the same starting position as for the Bench Press, except that you should use a narrow grip (from four to six inches between your index fingers) in the middle of the barbell.

3. The Movement—Keeping your upper arms motionless, bend your elbows and move the barbell in a semicircle from the starting position until it touches your forehead. Return the barbell along the same arc to the starting position and repeat.

4. Training Tip—This movement can also be done standing erect.

Lying Triceps Extension—start (above) and finish (below).

Nautilus Triceps Extension

1. Emphasis—This exercise places major stress on the triceps muscles at the back of your upper arms.

2. Starting Position—Adjust the seat of a Nautilus multi-triceps machine until you can sit in the machine with your shoulders level with the horizontal pad directly in front of them. Place your elbows on this pad, so that the outside of each elbow rests against the vertical pad at each end of the horizontal pad. Place the inside edges of your palms against the pads on the movement arms and then fully bend both arms.

3. The Movement—Slowly extend both arms fully. Pause for a count of two at the finish position. Lower back to the starting point, and repeat for the required number of repetitions.

4. Training Tip—As with the Nautilus Curl, this movement can be done with alternate arms. From the fully extended position, simply bend one arm completely and then re-extend it. Bend and extend the other arm, and continue alternating arms until your triceps are exhausted.

Nautilus Triceps Extension—start.

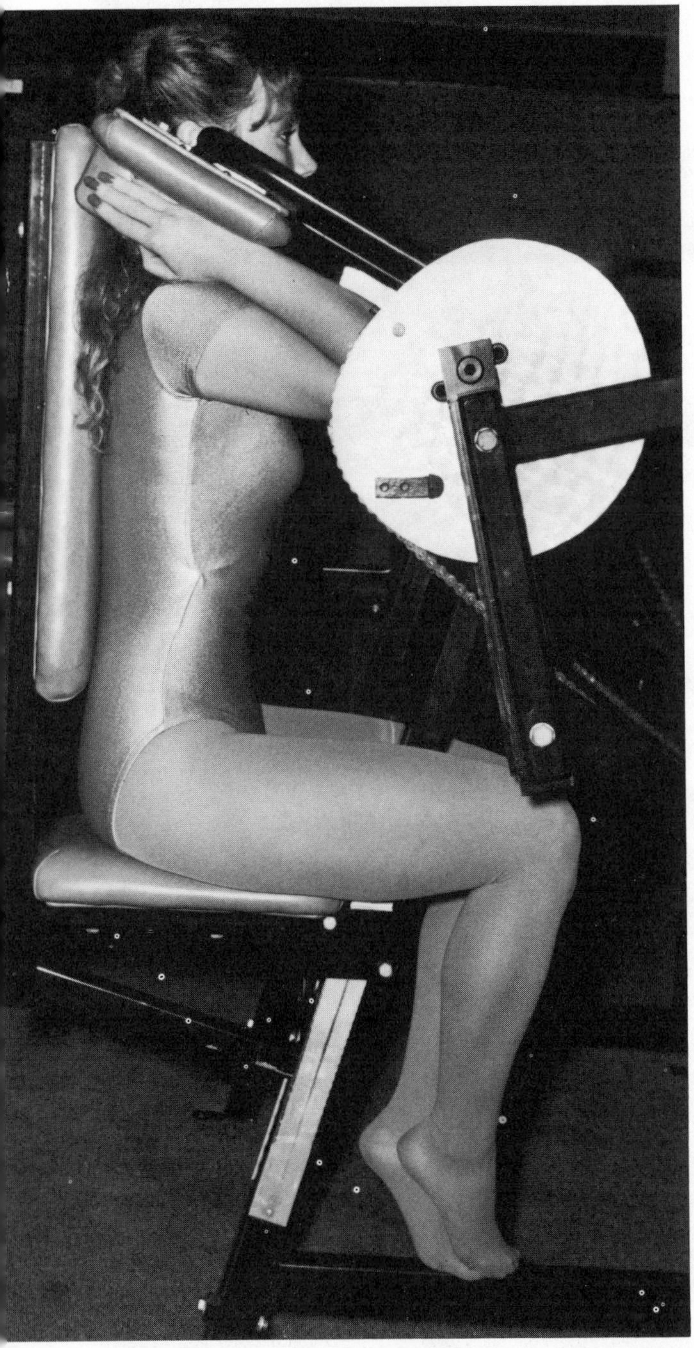

Nautilus Triceps Extension—finish.

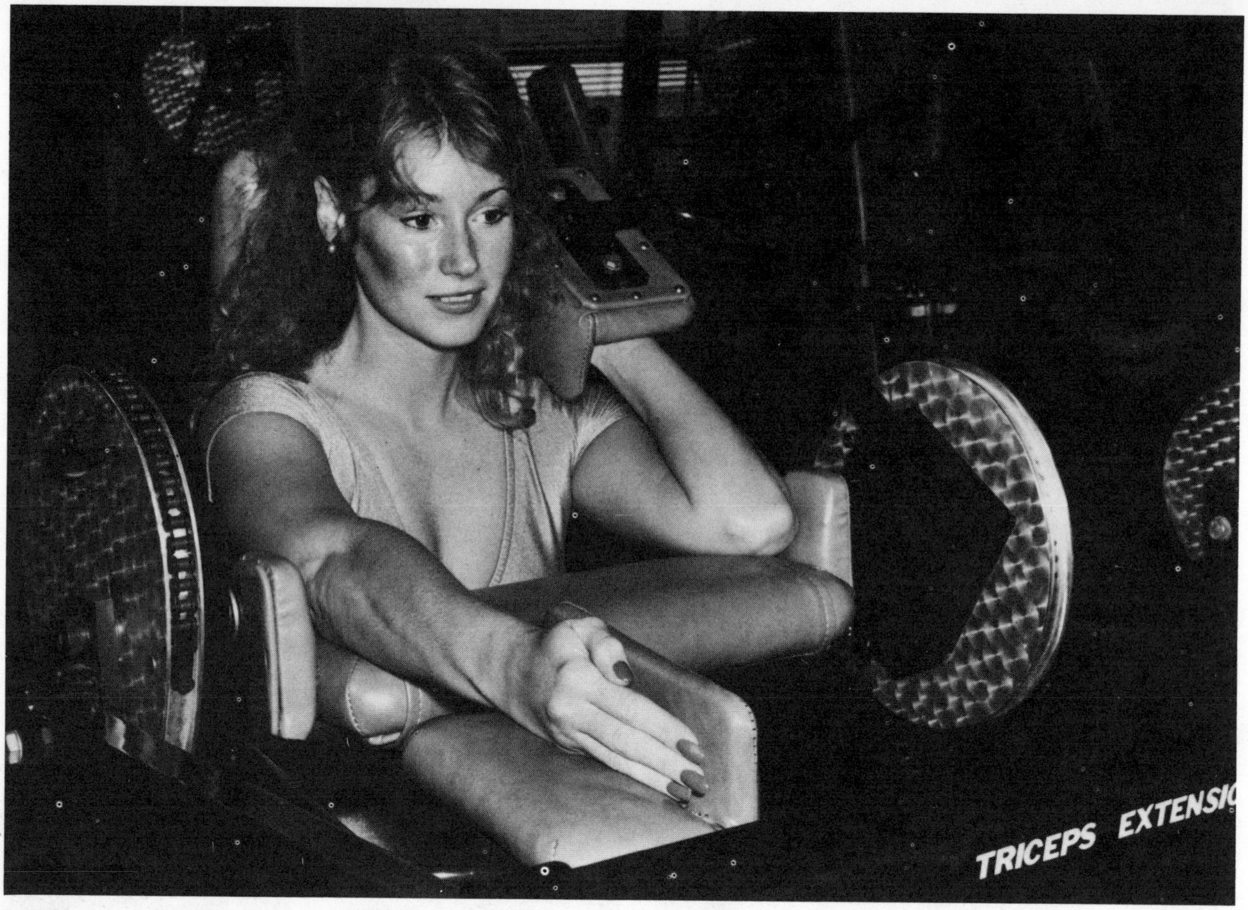

Nautilus Triceps Extension—finish, alternating right arm (above) and left arm (below).

Wrist Curl

1. Emphasis—This exercise places stress on all of the muscles of the forearm.

2. Starting Position—Sit at the end of a flat exercise bench with your feet set 10 to 12 inches apart. Take a grip 10 to 12 inches wide in the middle of a barbell handle, so your palms will face upward during the exercise. Run your forearms down your thighs so your wrists hang just off the front edges of your knees. Sag your fists down as far as possible by fully bending your wrists backward.

3. The Movement—From this starting position, curl your fists in small semicircles as high as possible by fully flexing your wrists. Return to the starting position, and repeat for the required number of repetitions.

4. Training Tips—When done with the palms facing upward during the movement, Wrist Curls stress the inner part of your forearm musculature. To place emphasis on the outer muscles of your forearm, do your Wrist Curls with your palms facing downward. With both variations of the Wrist Curl, you can make the movement more direct and concentrated by running your forearms along the top of a flat exercise bench instead of down your thighs.

Wrist Curl—start (below) and finish (right).

BEGINNING WORKOUTS

In the following three beginning workout programs, I have suggested starting weights for each exercise as a percentage of your body weight ("%"). So if you weigh 125 pounds and the exercise should be done with 20 percent of your body weight, you will be using 25 pounds as your starting weight.

These starting weights may feel either too light or too heavy for you, since individual women vary so widely in their native strength levels (due to such factors as body weight, age, and present degree of physical activity). If the weight is too heavy or light, simply adjust it downward or upward for your next workout.

Once past the beginning level, you will be familiar with your body's strength capabilities. Therefore, we will not list starting weights for any level past the first.

Wrist Curl with reversed grip—start (below).

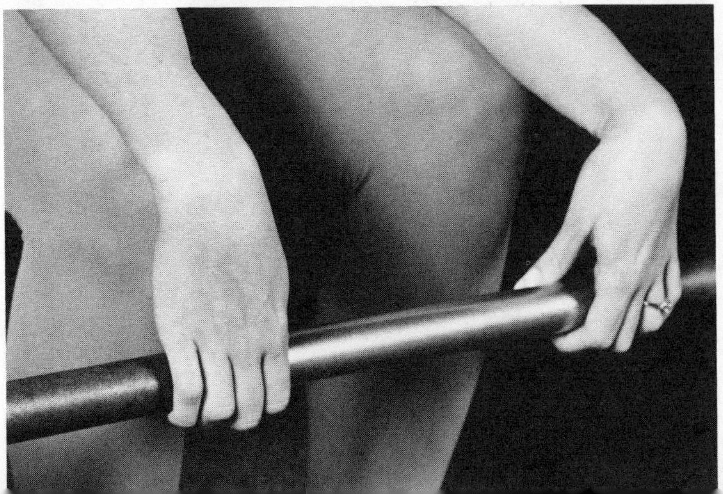

First Level Workouts

The programs laid out in Tables 3-1, 3-2, 3-3, and 3-4 are intended for use by rank beginners for the first four to six weeks of steady training. To be sure that you don't become unduly sore from your initial workouts, do only one set of each exercise for the first week. Then for the second week do two sets for those movements requiring two or more sets, and at the beginning of the third week, you can get up to the full program by adding a third set to all exercises requiring three sets.

Do all workouts three nonconsecutive days each week.

TABLE 3-1 Barbell Workout

Exercise	Sets	Reps	%
1. Situps	1-2	20-30	0
2. Standing Calf Raise	3	15-20	30
3. Squat	3	12-15	30
4. Barbell Bent Row	3	10-12	20
5. Bench Press	3	10-12	20
6. Military Press	2	8-10	15
7. Barbell Curl	2	8-10	12½
8. Lying Triceps Extension	2	8-10	12½
9. Wrist Curl	2	15-20	7½

TABLE 3-2 Universal Gym Workout

Exercise	Sets	Reps	%
1. Situps	1-2	20-30	0
2. Calf Press	3	15-20	40
3. Leg Press	3	12-15	40
4. Lat Pulldown	3	10-12	20
5. Bench Press	3	10-12	20
6. Seated Press	2	8-10	15
7. Pulley Curl	2	8-10	12½
8. Pulley Pushdown	2	8-10	12½

TABLE 3-3 Nautilus Workout

Exercise	Sets	Reps	%
1. Situps	1-2	20-30	0
2. Calf Press	3	15-20	40
3. Leg Press	2-3	12-15	40
4. Pullover	2-3	10-12	20
5. Bench Press	2-3	10-12	20
6. Seated Press	2	8-10	15
7. Curl	2	8-10	12½
8. Triceps Extension	2	8-10	12½

TABLE 3-4 Mixed-Equipment Workout

Exercise	Sets	Reps	%
1. Situps	1-2	20-30	0
2. Calf Press (Nautilus or Universal)	3	15-20	40
3. Squat (barbell)	3	12-15	30
4. Pullover (Nautilus)	2	10-12	20
5. Lat Pulldown (Nautilus or Universal)	2	10-12	20
6. Bench Press (barbell, Nautilus, or Universal)	3	10-12	20
7. Military Press (barbell)	2	8-10	15
8. Pulley Curl (Universal)	2	8-10	12½
9. Triceps Extension (Nautilus)	2	8-10	12½
10. Wrist Curl (barbell)	2	15-20	7½

Second Level Workouts

Depending on how quickly you progress in your training (which depends on how regularly and how hard you work out), you will be able to use the routines in this section during the period from about the six-week point of your training to the point where you've been working out for four to six months.

This low-intermediate level is the time when you begin to specialize toward particular goals by adapting your workouts to accomplish a variety of special types of conditioning. In this section, for example, we will give you unique training schedules for fitness and health, improved body contours, better sports performance, weight gaining, and slimming.

Fitness and Health

The best way to train with weights for physical fitness and health is through *circuit training*, the *aerobic* form of bodybuilding. In Chapter 2, we recommended doing all of the sets of each exercise in a training schedule before moving on to the next movement, which is the best method for building strength and muscle tissue. But to promote fitness and health, you should go completely through a routine—doing one set of each movement—for two or three full cycles.

In circuit training, we pick one or two exercises for each part of the body, or a total of 12 to 20 total movements. Then we go from one exercise to the next in a steady and methodical manner, averaging about one set per minute of training. And in this manner, we can attain the same type of aerobic effect as from running or swimming, but with the added benefit of being able to shape and tone the entire body, rather than just the legs or arms.

Circuits are usually set up around an entire gym, with equipment loaded to the correct exercise poundage before starting through a circuit. Using both free weights and a Universal Gym, Figure 3-1 shows a typical circuit training routine that you can use for two or three circuits.

Figure 3-1. Circuit-Training Routine

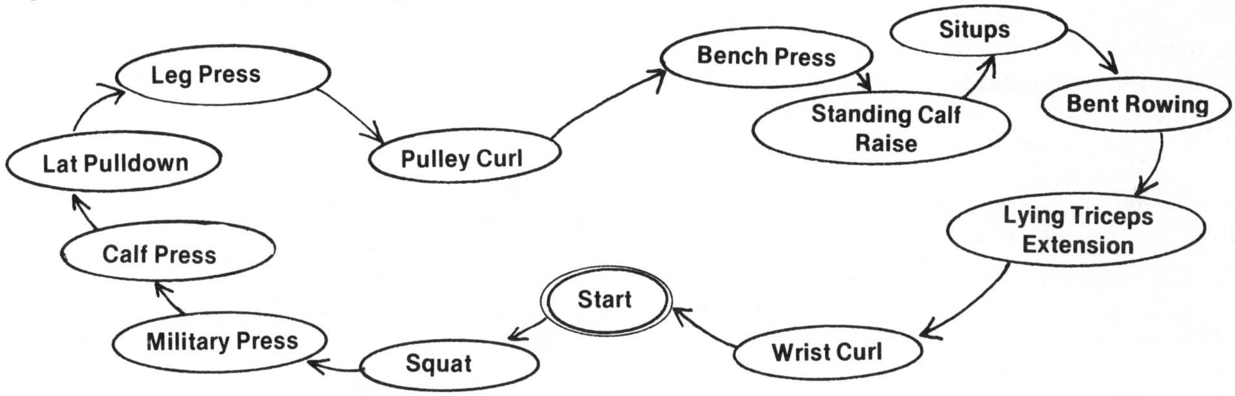

In busy gyms it is often difficult to set up a full 12- to 20-exercise circuit. In such a case, I recommend training with two to four shorter five- or six-exercise circuits. Such shorter circuits will effectively stimulate your body's cardiorespiratory system. Simply make two to three trips through each of the following sample circuits to see what I mean!

Circuit #1	Circuit #2
1. Leg Press	1. Squat
2. Pulley Curl	2. Wrist Curl
3. Bench Press	3. Military Press
4. Standing Calf Raise	4. Calf Press
5. Situps	5. Lat Pulldown
6. Bent Rowing	6. Lying Triceps Extension

Most Nautilus facilities have few—if any—free weights, but most automatically operate on a circuit-training philosophy. In order to run the maximum number of members through a program of exercise on Nautilus machines, the administrators of such clubs set up their facilities with the machines in long rows. Then members are required to begin at the start of a row and progress down it in order from one machine to the next, until finished.

While almost everyone associated with the Nautilus training concept will swear that one 20-minute circuit through their line of machines will result in optimum health, physical fitness, and muscle tone, we disagree. We feel you will need to make two trips through their circuits and perhaps even three trips. But with enough Nautilus work, you can and will improve your health and fitness.

Improved Appearance

One of the most wonderful things about bodybuilding with weights is the fact that it allows you to literally "sculpt" the body you desire. With progressive weight training and positively programmed nutrition, you can add or subtract curves anywhere on your body. You can slim your hips and thighs, add contour to your calves, firm your arms and back, and—within reason—you can even add shape and contour to your bustline.

With the exception of fatty breast tissue, all of a shapely woman's curves are caused by the size and contour of her skeletal muscles. A well-shaped *derriere*, for example, has for its foundation well-developed *gluteus maximus* muscles, over which is laid a covering of feminine fat. When the muscle tissue is nonexistent or if there is too much fat over the *gluteus maximus,* a woman's tush will look flat and shapeless.

To improve your body's shape and appearance, first decide which areas need the most work. Then simply do six to eight total sets for the muscles of that body part. As an example, let's take the thighs. To improve your thigh contour, try this routine:

1. Squats or Leg Press: 3 × 10–15 (three sets of 10 to 15 repetitions)
2. Leg Extensions: 2 × 10–15
3. Leg Curl: 3 × 10–15

Similarly, you can improve the contour of any other area simply by doing two or three exercises for it, totalling six to eight sets. And eventually—at the advanced level—you can do as many as 10 to 12 total sets for the muscle group(s) most needing improvement and four to six sets for each of the remaining muscle areas.

If you are too fat in some part of your body, it will be necessary to follow a lower-calorie diet in conjunction with your training if you wish optimum results. Exercise alone can improve the appearance of an overly fat body part by improving the muscle tone under the fat. But to attain complete results, you must combine sensible nutrition with your bodybuilding, to reduce the size of the fat deposits in the body part you are trying to improve.

With consistent training and dieting, you will notice results after only a week or two. And in two to three months, you should have reached your goals, unless you were initially very obese. Still, even the most obese woman can attain the figure she desires if she persistently and consistently trains and diets.

Every area of your body will respond fairly quickly to weight training and diet, except your bustline. Your breasts are largely composed of fatty tissues, with a thin underlying foundation of pectoral muscle. By training your pectorals hard and consistently with weights, you can improve the contour—and to some extent the size—of your breasts. But if Mother Nature did not give you a great deal of fatty tissue in your breasts, you will never be a Raquel Welch, short of cosmetic surgery. Bodybuilding can add to the muscle tissue in your chest, but not to the fatty breast tissues.

Improving Sports Performance

You can quickly and significantly improve your performance in any sport or physical recreation simply by weight training. And if you are a competing athlete, you can actually adopt a training regimen tailored specifically to your sport, which when conscientiously used *could* boost you to champion status.

In any sport, your body will perform with greater energy, strength, suppleness, and precision if it has been weight trained. You will, in point of fact, notice the difference after only two or three workouts!

In Table 3-5 you will find a good intermediate program using free weights to improve your athletic performance. (do all of the routines in this section three times per week).

TABLE 3-5 Free-Weight Intermediate Program

Exercise	Sets	Reps
1. Situps	3	25–50
2. Standing Calf Raise	4	15–20
3. Squat	4	10–15
4. Barbell Bent Row	4	8–12
5. Bench Press	4	8–12
6. Military Press	3	6–10
7. Barbell Curl	3	8–12
8. Lying Triceps Extension	3	8–12
9. Wrist Curl	3	15–20

Using a Universal Gym, you can try the intermediate-level sports improvement program laid out in Table 3-6.

TABLE 3-6 Universal Gym Intermediate Program

Exercise	Sets	Reps
1. Situps	3	25–50
2. Calf Press	4	15–20
3. Leg Press	4	10–15
4. Lat Pulldown	4	8–12
5. Bench Press	4	8–12
6. Seated Press	3	6–10
7. Pulley Curl	3	8–12
8. Pulley Pushdown	3	8–12

See Table 3-7 for an intermediate-level sports improvement routine using Nautilus machines.

TABLE 3-7 Nautilus Intermediate Program

Exercise	Sets	Reps
1. Situps	3	25–50
2. Calf Press	4	15–20
3. Leg Press	3	10–15
4. Pullover	2	8–12
5. Lat Pulldown	2	8–12
6. Bench Press	3	8–12
7. Seated Press	2	6–10
8. Curl	2	8–12
9. Triceps Extension	2	8–12

And if you are lucky enough to have access to all three types of resistance training equipment, you can use the intermediate-level sports improvement program in Table 3-8.

TABLE 3-8 Intermediate Program Using All Three Types of Resistance

Exercise	Sets	Reps
1. Situps	3	25-50
2. Calf Press (Universal or Nautilus)	4	15-20
3. Squat	4	10-15
4. Nautilus Pullover	2	8-12
5. Barbell Bent Row	2	8-12
6. Bench Press (Universal, Nautilus, or free weights)	4	8-12
7. Seated Press	3	6-10
8. Barbell Curl	3	8-12
9. Pulley Pushdown	3	8-12
10. Wrist Curl	3	15-20

It is beyond the scope of this book to outline specific weight training programs for every possible sport, so we will refer competitive athletes to either or both of two excellent books that contain such workouts for both men and women. These books are the *Gold's Gym Book of Strength Training* by Ken Sprague (J. P. Tracher, Inc., softcover, $8.95) and the *Complete Weight Training Book* by Bill Reynolds (Anderson-World Publications, softcover, $4.95). Both books are excellent sources of individualized sports improvement workouts with weights.

Weight Gaining

We receive a remarkable number of letters through our monthly magazines, *Muscle & Fitness* and *Shape,* from women seeking to gain weight. While there are no doubt fewer underweight women than obese women in North America, the thinner women seem to have an especially acute desire to normalize their appearance by gaining weight. For these women we have good news: By combining a specific nutritional approach with weight training, *anyone* can gain weight, even though some women will still gain rather slowly.

The nutritional secret is to eat frequently throughout the day—almost snacking constantly—rather than eating the traditional two or three large meals each day. Eating five or six times per day—and even more if you can!—allows your body to make more efficient use of the food you consume, because eating more frequently allows you to consume smaller quantities, which are more completely and easily digested. Eating five or six meals per day also allows you to comfortably increase your total daily caloric intake, which also helps you to gain weight.

Using this type of approach to your daily nutritional intake, here is a sample menu for one day of weight-gaining meals:

Meal One (8:00 a.m.)—eggs, bacon, fruit juice, food supplements (one Weider Good Life Multi-Pack, available in most health food stores).

Meal Two (10:30 a.m.)—cup of yogurt, raw nuts, glass of milk.

Meal Three (1:00 p.m.)—meat serving (beef, fish, chicken, turkey, lamb, or pork), baked potato, glass or two of milk.

Meal Four (3:30 p.m.)—tuna salad, glass of milk, food supplements (same as for Meal One).

Meal Five (6:00 p.m.)—meat serving, vegetable serving (your choice), rice, glass or two of milk.

Meal Six (8:30 p.m.)—protein shake (consisting of eight ounces of whole milk, two tablespoons of Weider Olympian milk-egg-yeast protein powder and fruit, all mixed for one to three minutes in a blender).

The key to gaining weight through exercise is to train with the heaviest possible weights on basic exercises (those that work two or more muscle groups in concert). The easiest way to do this is to *pyramid* your sets, which consists of adding weight to the bar or machine while reducing the number of repetitions with each succeeding set. To clarify this concept, here is a typical pyramid scheme:

Squat: 50 × 12 (50 lbs. for 12 reps)
60 × 10
70 × 8
80 × 6

Using this training philosophy, Table 3-9 presents a typical weight-gaining workout program using free weights. (Train three times per week; exercises to be pyramided are indicated with an asterisk).

With the Table 3-9 workout as an example, you will easily be able to formulate weight-gain routines using a Universal Gym, Nautilus machines, or a mixture of two (or all three) of the major forms of weight training.

Table 3-9 on next page.

TABLE 3-9 Weight-Gaining Workout Program

Exercise	Sets	Reps
1. Situps	2-3	25-50
2. Squat	4	12/10/8/6*
3. Barbell Bent Row	4	12/10/8/6*
4. Bench Press	4	12/10/8/6*
5. Military Press	3	10/8/6*
6. Barbell Curl	3	10/8/6*
7. Lying Triceps Extension	3	10/8/6*
8. Standing Toe Raise	4	15-20
9. Wrist Curl	3	15-20

* Pyramid these.

Slimming

As with weight gaining, you will achieve your best results when slimming with a combination of sensible nutrition and weight training. And if you are really serious about reducing your body's fat levels we recommend doing some type of aerobic activity for 20 to 30 minutes in between your bodybuilding-workout days.

It will be a slow process at best if you try to reduce your body fat levels without dieting. The most sensible diet is one about 20 percent lower in calories than what you normally eat. This, combined with an increase in daily physical activity, should trim off one or two pounds of fat per week.

The easiest way to reduce your caloric consumption by 20 percent is to avoid eating high-fat foods such as beef, pork, eggs, butter, full-fat milk, nuts, oils, and corn. By replacing fatty foods with protein and carbohydrates (fruit and vegetables), you automatically reduce your caloric intake, because one gram of fat yields nine calories when metabolized, versus the four calories yielded by either a gram of protein or a gram of carbohydrate.

The best form of weight training for slimming purposes is circuit training, discussed earlier in this chapter. Simply set up a circuit that will give you 30 to 50 total sets for your body each workout, and you will be well on the road to a slim and sleek new body.

If you are circuit training on Mondays, Wednesdays, and Fridays, you should walk, jog, bicycle, or swim for 20 to 30 minutes on Tuesdays, Thursdays, and Saturdays (a more thorough discussion of aerobic training is given in Chapter 4). Such aerobic activity will burn off extra calories, which will contribute to the new you—slender and beautiful!

INTERMEDIATE PROGRESSION

For the rest of your first four to six months of regular training, you should keep progressing in workout intensity by steadily adding resistance to the barbell or machine you use for every exercise in your routine. You should also occasionally add an extra set to each muscle group until you are doing a total of six to eight sets per body part. Then, at that point you will have reached the advanced level and will be ready to begin training more than three times per week.

UNIQUELY FEMALE QUESTIONS

Weight training during pregnancy, menstruation, and menopause are obviously unique, female problems in the bodybuilding life-style. Fortunately, progressive bodybuilding exercise and sensible nutritional practices can help any woman through these potentially trying times.

Scientific studies have shown that exercise before, during, and after pregnancy can ease physical problems (back pains, fatigue, etc.), shorten and ease labor, and make it easier to regain good physical condition and a sexy body after a baby is born.

Every woman should enter a pregnancy in the best possible physical condition. So if you are planning a family, both you and your husband should be conscious of your exercise and nutritional habits. Being strong, fit, and healthy simply reduces any risk associated with being pregnant and giving birth.

Under your physician's supervision, there is no reason why you should not continue bodybuilding through a full term of pregnancy. And there are many reason why you *should* continue bodybuilding. Studies show that physically active women experience less complications during their term, and they have a shorter and easier labor. Add in the weight-control and fatigue-lessening benefits of weight training—as well as its strengthening properties, which will relieve back discomfort—and any woman will conclude that regular exercise during pregnancy is essential!

As anyone who has gotten out of good physical condition and then tried to get back into shape can attest, it is a vey slow and painful process. Using pregnancy as an excuse to get out of condition and grow fat is, therefore, merely condemning yourself to a life of obesity or to several hard months of training and dieting. So, the best bet is to stay in shape and control your weight while you are pregnant. That way, you'll be back to your youthful pre-pregnancy appearance in only a few short weeks.

All women face some sort of menstrual complication sometime during their lives. These include cramps, depression, nausea, breast tenderness, and headaches. Since most of these problems are either caused or aggravated by poor dietary and exercise practices, adopting a bodybuilding life-style can spare you many of the discomforts of menstruation.

Physically active women often tell us how dramatically their menstrual problems have been reduced once they've undertaken a regular exercise program. One reason for this is the tension-relieving function of exercises. Also, exercise "oxygenates" the body and strengthens the lower torso muscles. Both of these functions will reduce menstrual complications, especially cramps.

If you suffer a lot from cramps and depression, it's probably because your body becomes mineral-deficient during your menstrual cycle. Menstruation significantly elevates the body's need for all minerals, but particularly for iron, potassium, and calcium. You should find relief from cramping and depression by simply taking three to five chelated multiple-mineral tablets or capsules per day, beginning five to seven days before your period begins and continuing until two to three days after it ceases.

Menopausal symptoms can also be greatly relieved simply by adopting good exercise and nutritional habits. These symptoms are caused by changes in the levels of a woman's various hormonal secretions, and studies have shown that regular exercise and healthy eating habits normalize hormonal balances enough at this trying time to greatly reduce menopausal complications, the same as they reduce menstrual problems and pregnancy complications!

ONWARD

In the next chapter, you will be introduced to a number of intermediate- and advanced-level training techniques. And then in Chapter 5, you will add 24 new movements to the exercise pool started in this chapter.

April Nicotra, three-time winner of the Ms. Eastern America title, does an advanced bodybuilding exercise, Cable Crossovers.

4

Intermediate/Advanced Training Techniques

In this chapter we will expand your knowledge of bodybuilding-training strategies by discussing such intermediate and advanced techniques as how to combine aerobic activities with weight training; power training; advanced nutrition; the use of training partners; overtraining and staleness; how to smash past sticking points; the prevention and treatment of injuries; how to make up your own training routines; where to find additional sources of information about bodybuilding and weight training; and how to keep progressing as a potential competitive bodybuilder.

AEROBICS AND WEIGHT TRAINING

As mentioned in Chapter 3, you will be able to achieve remarkable results in changing your physical appearance by combining weight training with aerobic activity. And by combining these two forms of physical training, you will be building health, better physical appearance, and drastically improved physical fitness.

The best way to combine weight training with aerobic activity is to do each on alternate days, e.g., weight train on Mondays, Wednesdays, and Fridays and aerobic workouts on Tuesdays, Thursdays, and Saturdays. You can either use Sunday as a fourth aerobic workout day, or you can spend Sundays resting fully from physical activity or doing some other form of recreation, such as sailing, hiking, or camping.

The key in all physical activity—whether it is for building strength or increasing endurance—is *regularity*. You will need to exercise only 30 to 60 minutes per day for optimum results when trying to improve your strength and appearance, *if* you do it regularly. With the exception of Sundays, you should never miss an exercise day, regardless of what social or business commitments you might have. You will always be able to find 30 to 60 minutes for a workout, even if you must get up a half hour earlier each day.

Aerobic activity is low-intensity exercise carried on for a prolonged period of time. The intensity has to be low enough for the body to supply all the oxygen needed to prolong the activity. If the intensity is too high, the work becomes anaerobic, and the body can't take in enough oxygen to cover what is being used up.

And as a result, the body goes quickly into oxygen debt and exercise must be ceased.

Aerobic exercise produces a heightened level of physical endurance. It is also a superior way to burn off excess calories, which melts away the body's fat desposits. Interestingly, aerobic exercise actually burns more calories than an equivalent amount of more intense anaerobic exercise.

The key to choosing aerobic activities for your training is finding those that you can continue doing for 30 to 40 minutes. And a second key is to pick activities that you enjoy doing, because exercise should never be a chore.

Statistically, running is America's favorite aerobic activity. Over 25 million Americans run on at least a sporadic basis. The advantages of running are: (1) It's a superior form of aerobic activity; (2) it's inexpensive; and (3) almost anyone can do it. Essentially, all you need are a good pair of running shoes, a physical exam (with a stress test if you're over 40 years of age), and the great outdoors.

There is one drawback to running that you should be aware of, however. Every time your foot strikes the turf or pavement, the feet, ankles, knees, and hips are stressed. And this often causes injuries, which can be avoided by swimming, bicycling, or participating in other aerobic activities in which some or all of the body weight is supported by the water or by some apparatus you're using to exercise.

There are several fine books on running, and rather than write another one, we recommend that you buy one or two books for tips on beginning a program of regular running. One of the best books for all experience levels is *Jog, Run, Race* by Joe Henderson.

Walking is a less intense activity than running, so it's more suitable to older individuals or to someone who has had injuries to her legs. Still, walking is as effective as running, because the key to caloric consumption is the distance covered on foot, not the speed at which it is covered. A two-mile walk—even though it takes two or three times as long to complete—burns the same number of calories as a two-mile run.

Swimming is a popular and orthopedically safe aerobic activity, although one that can be considerably more expensive than running or walking. When swimming, the water totally supports your body, so the risk of leg-muscle and joint injuries is almost nonexistent.

While bicycling presents some risk in terms of cycle crashes, it is also an orthopedically safe activity. And bicycling is zooming in popularity in the United States. Look around you any weekend, and you'll see whole families out for long rides on their bikes. As a rough rule of thumb, two miles of bicycling is about equivalent to a mile of running or walking in terms of the calories burned while exercising.

Sheila Byrd combines her weight-training routines with swimming.

Racquet sports—particularly tennis and racquetball—are popular aerobic activities, although somewhat inferior to steady-state work like running and bicycling. Stopping and starting gives the heart and circulatory system a good workout, of course, but subjects a woman's legs to tremendous stresses. And the expense of equipment and court time can mount up quite rapidly.

Numerous other aerobic activities exist, and you can perhaps find one that will benefit you more than any that we've discussed. For a fuller listing of activities and a deeper appreciation of aerobic conditioning, we'd suggest that you consult Dr. Kenneth Cooper's *Aerobics* book.

Once you have chosen an aerobic activity suitable to your fitness needs and personality, the key becomes regularity. In your program you should never miss an aerobic workout, which means you must do three or four such sessions per week.

A second key is duration of exercise. To achieve an aerobic effect (that is, to improve your fitness), you must elevate your heart rate above 130 beats per minute, and then keep it there for a minimum of 15 minutes. This is the *minimum*, and we recommend that you gradually increase this minimum up to a level of 30 to 40 minutes of continuous aerobic activity per training day.

So, this is the first of three important factors (aerobics, diet, and weight training) in reaching your fitness and appearance goals. Go slowly, go for a long period of time, and never miss an aerobic session. Adhering to these rules will quickly bring you maximum benefits from your aerobic workouts.

POWER TRAINING

If your goal is to become extremely strong, you should begin at this point to specialize specifically on developing maximum strength. This is done by doing workouts of low-rep, heavy-resistance training on basic exercises.

Maximum strength is not a function of muscle mass, although there *is* usually a direct relationship between the size of a muscle group and the amount of weight you can use for four to eight reps on a movement for that body part. Instead, maximum power is a function of contractile strength (your ability to contract a great number of individual muscle fibers) and the toughness or strength of your connective tissues (tendons, ligaments, and cartilages).

These two qualtities are best developed by using low-rep (one to five reps) sets on basic exercises like the Squat, Bench Press, and Deadlift. At this point you will be ready to train like this more than three days per week by using a four-day split routine (see the following section of this chapter for more detailed information on split routines). This involves training half of the body one day and half the next, then resting for a day or two before repeating the cycle.

Following the principles outlined so far, Table 4-1 presents a free-weight routine you can use to develop maximum power. (Note: pyramid your sets, reps, and weights on those exercises marked with an asterisk.)

TABLE 4-1 Free-Weight Power Routine

Exercise	Sets	Reps
Monday-Thursday		
1. Situps	3	25-50
2. Squat	5	5/4/3/2/2*
3. Deadlift	3	5/3/2*
4. Barbell Bent Row	4	6/5/4/4*
5. Shrug	3	6-8
6. Barbell Curl	4	6/5/4/3*
7. Wrist Curl	3	8-10
8. Standing Calf Raise	5	10-12
Tuesday-Friday		
1. Leg Raise	3	25-50
2. Bench Press	5	5/4/3/2/2*
3. Incline Press	3	5/4/3*
4. Military Press	4	5/4/3/2*
5. Lying Triceps Extension	4	4/4/3/3*
6. Reverse Wrist Curl	3	8-10
7. Seated Calf Raise	5	10-12

* Pyramid these.

Five exercises in this routine are described and illustrated in Chapter 5, so please refer to that chapter for correct exercise form for these movements. The exercises explained in Chapter 5 are the Incline Press, Deadlift, Shrug, Leg Raise, and Seated Calf Raise.

Using this free-weight routine as an example of how to power train, you can easily develop workouts for maximum strength development using a Universal Gym or the various Nautilus machines. Overall, however, we think you'll find it best to do your power workouts primarily with free weights. There are several reasons for this, particularly the variety of exercises you can do with free weights and the fact that *you* control

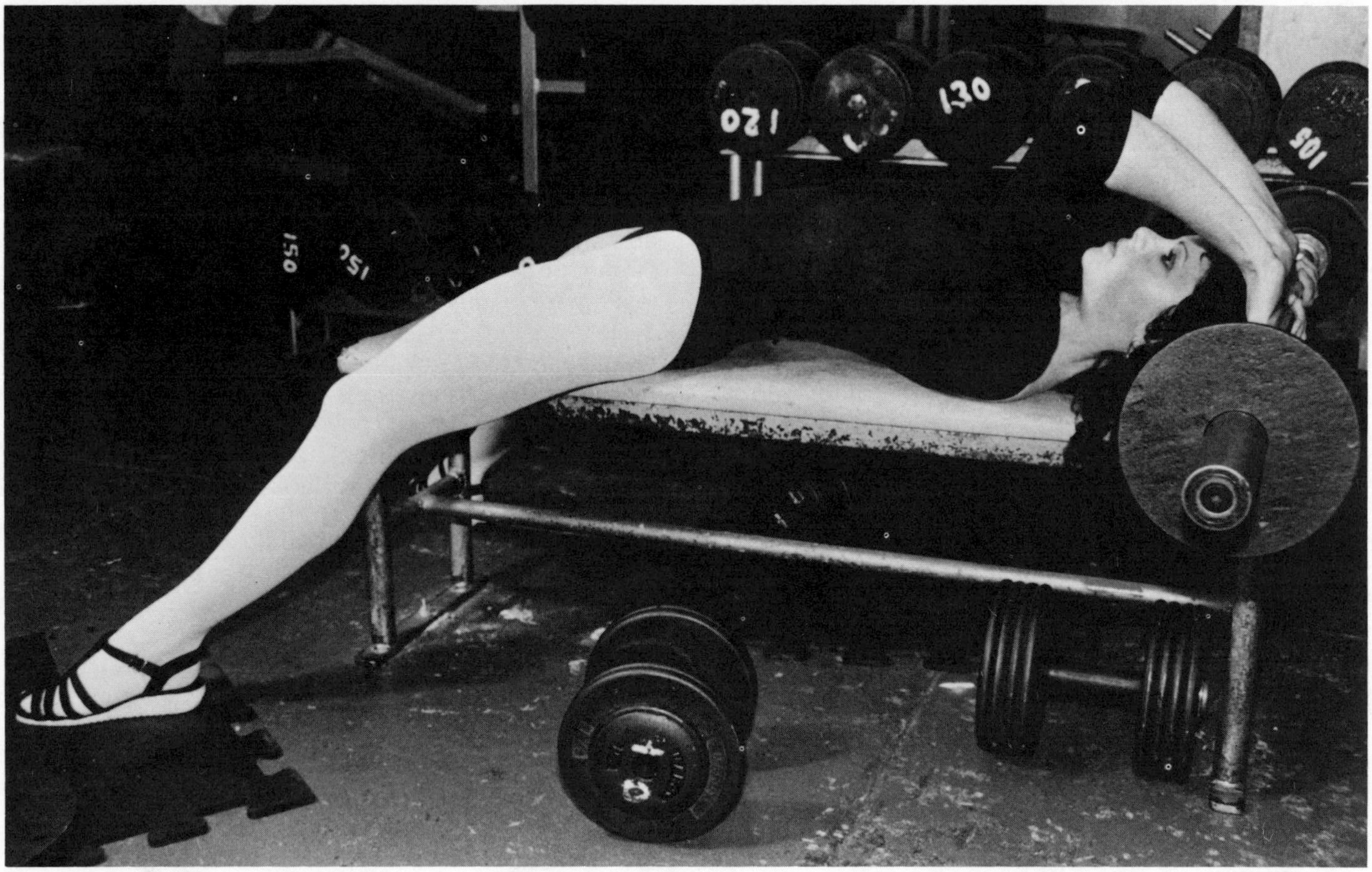

World champion bodybuilder, Lisa Lyon, demonstrates excellent form in Lying Triceps Extension.

the weight when using a barbell or dumbbell in your workout.

While machines are fine for building a degree of strength, body tone, and muscle shape, free weights are far less expensive to use and much more effective. When using free weights, *you* control the movement, while with machines, the *machine* controls it for you. And with Nautilus and Universal Gym machines, the number of exercises that you can do for each body part is severely limited, usually to only two or three movements. In contrast, you can do *hundreds* of exercises for each body part with free weights.

SPLIT ROUTINES

At the beginning level of training, part of the manner in which we increased the intensity of your workouts was to gradually add to the total number of sets you did for each body part. While this *is* an effective method of increasing training intensity, it quickly becomes difficult to complete a routine with a high number of sets for the entire body in one workout. With a large number of sets, you simply run out of energy before you can do justice in your workout to every body part.

So, once you've gotten to the point where you are doing more than six to eight total sets for each muscle group, it's a good idea to begin doing only a part of the body or muscle group in each workout. This way you will have a greater amount of energy to devote to each muscle group.

In a split routine, we divide the body up into two or three sections and train these sections four to six days per week. The most basic split routine—and the one you should use at the intermediate level—divides the body in half and trains each half twice per week, a total of four weekly workouts. Here are two examples of how such a four-day split routine works:

Routine A

Monday-Thursday	Tuesday-Friday
Chest	Thighs
Shoulders	Back
Triceps	Biceps
Forearms	Neck
Calves	Calves
Abdominals	Abdominals

Routine B

Monday-Thursday	Tuesday-Friday
Chest	Thighs
Back	Biceps
Shoulders	Triceps
Forearms	Calves
Calves	Abdominals
Abdominals	

The next step up the split routine ladder of intensity is to a five-day split. In such a split routine, the body is still divided into halves, with the halves trained on alternate days Monday through Friday. Designating the two halves of such a split routine *A* and *B*, Table 4-2 shows how such a routine works.

TABLE 4-2 How a Five-Day Split Works

Week	Mon.	Tues.	Wed.	Thurs.	Fri.
One	A	B	A	B	A
Two	B	A	B	A	B

Moving up to training on a six-day-per-week split routine, there are two intensity levels you can work with. In the first of these, the body is split into three sections, and each is trained twice a week, see Table 4-3. (Calves and abdominals can be trained daily.)

TABLE 4-3 How a Six-Day Split Works

Mon.-Thurs.	Tues.-Fri.	Wed.-Sat.
Chest	Back	Thighs
Shoulders	Biceps	Triceps
Forearms	Calves	Calves
Calves	Abdominals	Abdominals
Abdominals		

In the final type of split routine, you still train six days per week, but you do each body part three times per week. In this case, the body is split into two halves—as in a four-day split routine—with one half worked on Mondays, Wednesdays, and Fridays and the other half trained on Tuesdays, Thursdays, and Saturdays.

Essentially, the main purpose of a split routine is to allow you to do shorter workouts. That way, you can work much harder on every muscle group, instead of running out of energy toward the end of a long three-day-per-week training routine. And if you can train all of your muscle groups harder, you will make much faster progress!

TRAINING PARTNERS

Bodybuilding training is an excellent activity to share with someone. And it's a good idea to use a training partner if you are preparing for bodybuilding competition, when you must be pushing extremely hard in your workouts to bring out the ultimate in muscle mass and muscular definition.

While bodybuilding serves well as a solitary activity—and many women prefer to to keep it that way—the rests between sets are natural conversation breaks. You will probably find that a training session will become much more enjoyable and go by more quickly when you share it with a good friend.

In the past few years, it's become very fashionable for a woman to weight train with her husband or boyfriend. A hundred years ago in America, men and women shared physical labor, which in turn strengthened their marriages. But today there are too few opportunities for a man and woman to break a good old-fashioned sweat together. Bodybuilding together is one of the few ways to do this, and we are sure you will develop a whole new concept of togetherness if you train regularly with the man in your life.

When a woman is preparing for bodybuilding competition, she must push every set of every exercise to the limit. This can be dangerous at times, because when a bodybuilder pushes a set to failure, she can be pinned under a weight. Then, a partner becomes essential to safe training. And at the end of a set, your training partner can also help you to just complete a set by lifting up a little on the bar. Such a forced rep is extremely valuable to a competing bodybuilder, and it couldn't be done without a training partner.

ADVANCED NUTRITION

Bodybuilding and good nutritional practices go well together. It seems impossible to take

Whether working with weights or working on a machine, a training partner can help you get the most out of a workout, providing encouragement as well as preventing injury.

care of your body by exercising it regularly, without thinking about taking care of it by also feeding it the best foods available.

At the most basic level, we *are* what we eat. Every cell in the human body is made up from the nutrients that we take in, so it makes good sense to eat only the highest-quality foods.

The human body is a very remarkable organic system, within which every external stimulus evokes from the body a distinct physical response. Eat trashy, fatty, and devitalized foods, for example, and your body will grow weak and fat as a response. But eat natural, wholesome, and vital foods, and your body grows strong, healthy, and lean.

In Chapter 2 we discussed the basic health-promoting diet and outlined several rules of sound nutition. Now we will go into the study of nutrition more specifically.

You needn't be a biochemist to understand the basics of diet and nutrition, but to be sure that you put the right foods into your diet it will be necessary to develop a thorough knowledge of nutrition. Therefore, we suggest that you read all of the nutrition books and articles available to you, particularly the articles in our monthly magazines, *Shape* and *Muscle* & *Fitness*. From the starting point of this book's nutrition discussions, you can then build a thorough working knowledge of healthy nutritional practices.

There are six fundamental food nutrients—protein, fats, carbohydrates, vitamins, minerals, and water. And for optimum health, these nutrients must be carefully balanced in the human diet. This is because many foods are catalytic, or will function correctly only in combination with other nutrients. Some vitamins, for example, are only assimilated completely in the presence of certain minerals.

On a purely caloric basis, the National Research Council recommends that 58 percent of your diet consist of carbohydrates, 30 percent of fats, and 12 percent of proteins. The average woman needs one gram of good quality protein for each kilogram (2.2 pounds) of her body weight. Therefore, a 125-pound woman needs a little less than 60 grams of protein per day in her diet.

The highest quality proteins come from animal sources. These are milk, eggs, beef, poultry, fish, and lamb. By far the best sources are milk and eggs, so be sure to include in your diet at least one serving of each of these foods per day. Or, more conveniently, you can make up the milk-egg-yeast protein shake described in the previous chapter and drink one or two shakes per day.

Generally speaking, vegetable sources of protein are inferior to animal sources, because they lack one or more of the eight essential amino acids. Amino acids are the basic components of proteins. There are 22 amino acids, of which the body can manufacture 14. The remaining eight—the essential amino acids—must be taken into the body in the foods we eat. Animal proteins are high in these eight essential amino acids, while vegetable sources aren't.

By intelligently combining vegetable protein sources with either milk or other vegetable proteins, however, you can greatly enhance the amino acid balance in a vegetarian diet. These are the best food combinations:

1. Grains and milk products
2. Grains and legumes
3. Seeds and legumes

Looking at these combinations, you can easily see that various ethnic groups around the world have been intuitively combining these foods for centuries. This is why rice and beans are a staple food combination in many countries, and why we Americans seem to crave a glass of milk with a peanut butter sandwich, or why we like milk on cereal. Very simply put, the human body is capable of telling us what we should be eating, if we can only learn to interpret its signals.

Carbohydrates, nature's sugars, are greatly misunderstood by most people in America. Due to the popularity of low-carbohydrate diets such as the Dr. Atkins and the Dr. Stillman diets, most people fear that carbohydrates will make a person fat. This is simply not true, since the only thing that makes a woman fat is systematically eating too many calories. And when you are on a low-calorie diet, you actually need to eat carbohydrates for optimum weight loss!

The majority of your carbohydrate intake should be from complex carbohydrates, the type of sugars found in nature, versus simple carbohydrates, which have been refined and processed. Fruits, vegetables, and grains are the best sources of complex carbohydrates. You should avoid such simple carbohydrates as white sugar and white flour.

Keeping within your body's daily caloric tolerances, you should eat at least 150 grams of carbohydrate per day. Of this quantity, you will need about 75 grams of carbohdyrate just for your body's basic metabolic needs, particularly for proper brain function, which is conducted almost exclusively on carbohydrate sugars. You will need an additional 75 to 100 grams of carbohydrate per day for your body's energy needs.

Because they are broken down quickly in the human body, carbohydrates are good for quick energy, such as when you find yourself dragging in the later afternoon, or when you need energy for a workout. It's difficult, however, to keep a steady flow of energy in your body with carbohydrates. To do so, you'd need to eat a small amount of carbohydrate every 20 to 30 minutes. Therefore, we also must eat some fats, which are used more slowly for energy, and which result in a sustained release of energy.

There are two types of fats—saturated fats (found in coconut oil and all animal fats) and unsaturated fats (found in almost all vegetable oils). A certain amount of fat in the diet is natural and healthy, but a high fat intake—particularly of saturated fats—has been positively identified as contributing to heart and vascular disease.

Since fats yield more than twice the number of calories per gram than is yielded by protein and carbohydrates, it's a wise move to limit fat consumption, particularly when you are trying to lose body fat. The fats that you do ingest should be about two-thirds from vegetable sources and one-third from animal sources.

Vitamins and minerals are catalysts of all the body's biochemical functions. Therefore, they must be present in the human diet, although not to the extent proposed by many food faddists. All you need to do to supply your body with an optimum and balanced level of vitamins and minerals is to take one or two Weider Good Life multiple vitamin-mineral packs per day!

In summary, your body will become even more healthy and fit if you combine good nutritional practices with your bodybuilding training. Hand-in-hand, good nutrition and regular exercise can turn you into a super woman!

OVERTRAINING

While you will make better progress by increasing the volume of your workouts at the beginning and intermediate levels of training, it is possible to do too much work and *overtrain*. Once the fine line between an optimum training load and one that induces overtraining has been crossed, your body will break down on you. At the very least, you will lose all desire for additional training. At the worst, you will incur an injury or become ill with a cold or the flu.

Overtraining is usually caused by workouts that are too long, not too intense. There is an overall energy drain greater than what the body can normally replace. As with your bank account, your body writes more checks that it can cover, and it goes "broke" by overtraining.

The secret, then, to prevent overtraining is to train with less total sets per body part, but with greater intensity (with heavier weights or shorter rest intervals). And if you begin to feel loggy, lazy in the gym, or chronically fatigued, you can head off an overtraining breakdown by taking a week's layoff from training, and then starting back with shorter, more intense workouts.

STICKING POINTS

The human body gains cyclically, or in spurts, with dormant periods lasting from one week to as much as six months. Such long *sticking points* can be so discouraging that many women quit bodybuilding. And this is unfortunate, because all sticking points can be eliminated almost as soon as they become evident.

Most sticking points occur when your body becomes too used to the training program you are following. It adapts so well to workout stimuli that it no longer needs to respond by adapting to the stimuli.

When this happens, you can start progressing again almost immediately by simply changing to a totally new routine. Then the new stimulus is so unexpected by the body that it is *forced* to respond, and you begin again to make good progress in your workouts.

To prevent sticking points, you should switch training routines at least once each four to six weeks. Some bodybuilders change their training programs weekly, or even daily to avoid sticking points. Either way, the key is to change the stimulus you give your body, which then is forced to make a renewed physical response.

INJURIES

Minor injuries are inevitable in any physical activity that's carried on regularly for long periods of time. In bodybuilding, these injuries usually consist of mildly strained muscles, but occasionally more serious muscle tears or joint injuries can occur, particularly if a spotter isn't standing by when very heavy weights are being used in a workout.

Most bodybuilding-related injuries can be prevented simply by warming up thoroughly, and then staying warm during the workout. To keep from cooling off, never rest more than 90 seconds between sets. A majority of training injuries we've dealt with occurred when a student had spent 10 to 15 minutes talking with someone in the gym and them jumped back into the middle of a workout.

If you do sustain a serious training injury, consult your family physician and follow his directions explicitly. If your injury is mild, however, you can begin home treatment of it by resting the injured area for three to five days, or until soreness disappears. After 48 hours, you can apply heat to the injured area several times each day to hasten the healing process.

After an injury has healed, start training again by doing one or two very light sets of basic exercises that put stress on the injured area. Then take three to five workouts to build back up to your previous training intensity, backing off in your progression immediately when you feel pain in the injured area. If you follow these guidelines, the injured part will regain its strength and will often end up even stronger than before the injury.

When you've been badly injured in a sport or some type of a car or home accident—even if surgery was required to repair the damaged muscle or joint—you can rehabilitate the injury by following the same intensity progression in your workouts as outlined above. By using weights, atrophied muscles can be restored to full strength very quickly, and injured joints can be rehabilitated far more rapidly than with conventional physical therapy.

INDIVIDUALIZING YOUR OWN ROUTINE

While there are numerous excellent training routines outlined in this book, you will eventually outgrow them and come to the point where you will want to make up your own weight-training programs. By then, you will have developed a good feel for what exercises and types of training routines work best for your own unique body. Armed with that "instinct" and the following guidelines, you will have no trouble formulating your own individualized workouts.

Here are five guidelines that you should use when making up a new training program:

1. Stay within your limits. At the intermediate level do up to six to eight total sets per muscle group, and at the advanced level, do ten to twelve total sets for each body part. Once you get past doing six to eight sets per body part, switch to a split routine.
2. Do your abdominal training first in your workout as an added warm-up for the heavier training to follow.
3. Always do your torso (chest, back, and shoulders) workouts *before* you train your arms. Always do any forearm training *after* you have finished the rest of your body.
4. Train the larger muscle groups first. In order from largest to smallest groups, your body consists of thighs, back, chest, calves, deltoids, biceps-triceps, forearms, and abdominal muscles.
5. For each body part, be sure to do at least one basic exercise (working two or more muscle groups in concert, e.g. the Bench Press, Squat, or Bent Row) and one isolation movement (working only the one muscle group, e.g., Concentration Curls, Side Laterals, or Pulley Pushdowns). Do the basic exercise(s) first, followed by the isolation movement(s).

ADDITIONAL INFORMATION

You could undoubtedly train with weights for the rest of your life armed only with the information in this book. But if you have a questing mind, you will no doubt want to know *everything* about the activity you love. If this is the case, you will need a listing of sources of additional information about weight training and bodybuilding.

There are numerous books on the market treating these activities thoroughly, and they are listed in the Bibliography at the end of this book. Unfortunately, there are not very many books dealing directly with women's training, but there are few inherent differences between men and women involved in weight training, so the information in male-oriented bodybuilding books will also apply to you.

Numerous bodybuilding and weight-training magazines are available. All give good information and instruction, but the best bodybuilding magazine is *Muscle & Fitness*, which we publish. It is truly the Bible of weight training and bodybuilding. And you might also be interested in reading our new women's self-improvement magazine, *Shape,* which is quickly gaining a reputation to equal that of *Muscle & Fitness.*

Many champion male and female bodybuilders offer a series of training courses, which they advertise in *Muscle & Fitness.* Generally speaking, these courses are a fair supplement to books like this, so you might want to invest in one or two sets of courses.

Mandy Tanny: "If you don't train hard, you just won't get results."

Out of the realm of the written word, one of the best sources of additional information about weight training and bodybuilding is your peers, the people with whom you train. Both male and female bodybuilders are a friendly and gregarious lot, and they positively *love* to help less experienced trainees with their problems. Simply determine who has the information you need, and then *ask* for it!

Finally, you may have the rare opportunity of attending the training seminar of a champion bodybuilder. You'll be exposed to an incredible array of new and useful information at such seminars, even at those conducted by famous male bodybuilders. These seminars are conducted all over the country, and they're invariably advertised on a gym bulletin board for a few weeks before the event. The cost for training seminars ranges from about 10 to 30 dollars, and they're worth every cent.

PROGRESSING AS A COMPETITIVE BODYBUILDER

If competitive bodybuilding is your ultimate goal, what you do with your mind and body through the intermediate and advanced training levels will make or break you once you reach competitive condition. The most important thing to watch is that your bodily proportions stay in balance. Weak body parts—usually the calves, back or arms—cause more women bodybuilders to lose contests than any other physical fault. Such weaknesses usually show up first during the intermediate training phase and then are neglected during the advanced phase until it becomes almost impossible to bring a lagging body part up to the level of the rest of the body.

So, above all else, try as hard as you can to balance your bodily proportions. Seek a critical evaluation from someone in your gym, who has the ability to analyze body proportions. Usually this will be a former or current competitor, and most gyms have one or more such men or women.

Once you have identified potential weak points, focus the bulk of your mental and physical energies on them until they have become strong points. *Specialize* on your weaknesses by putting full mental concentration on every rep of every set of every exercise for a lagging body part. And constantly strive to use greater intensity in each exercise you do for a weak muscle group.

If you have an especially weak body part, use the Weider *Muscle Priority* principle on it by training that muscle group first in your workout. Only then can you focus your maximum mental and physical energies on training a weak point. Later in a workout you will undoubtedly be too fatigued to give 100 percent effort to training *any* muscle group, let alone one that's not progressing as fast as it should.

While balancing your bodily proportions should be uppermost in your mind during the intermediate and advanced training phases, you should also be concerned about gradually adding muscle mass to your body. Just be sure that you don't get so carried away with adding mass that you allow your proportions to suffer.

It's always a great temptation to spend most of your time training those muscle groups that respond easily, because you can really *see* the gains. But rationally, it's far better to focus the bulk of your energies on those groups that grow most slowly, because only then will you come close to possessing ideal bodily proportions.

If you train regularly and with reasonable intensity, muscle mass will come with time. But you must be patient, because it will require three to five years of persistent training to be ready to win a title. Rome wasn't built in a day, and neither will be the body of a champion woman bodybuilder!

Throughout the intermediate and advanced levels, you should be experimenting with the widest possible variety of training and nutritional philosophies, using the Weider *Instinctive Training* principle to decide what works best on your unique body. This principle encompasses a bodybuilder's ability to recognize and correctly interpret the biofeedback her body gives her.

As an example, if you experience muscle soreness a day after a training session, you will know that you had an especially good workout. And if you feel a good *pump* (a tight, blood-congested feeling in a muscle group, cause by an influx of blood to clear away fatigue by-products and refuel a working muscle), you will also know you trained the pumped body part to its maximum.

By constantly experimenting, you can discover over the course of two or three years exactly what training techniques and diets work best for you. And then—even though you will always be seeking better ways to do things—you will be able to train and diet correctly enough for your body to make optimal muscle gains.

In your nutritional experiments, focus on discovering what combinations and quantities of food supplements give you the best muscle growth rates. While one or two Weider Good Life multiple vitamin-mineral packs per day will be adequate food supplementation for the average person, bodybuilders and competing athletes train so hard and are under such prolonged stress that they need greater amounts of vitamins and minerals

The problem in developing an individualized supplement schedule is that everyone needs different amounts of vitamins and minerals. Your task is to find out what dosages and combinations of supplements work best for you. And it could take years to find out what really works best inside your unique body.

Start your experiments by taking an individual vitamin or mineral—e.g., vitamin C—with varying dosage levels. Does 1000 mg. give you better training energy and recuperation than 500 mg.? Or, do you need 2000 mg.? Take each individual vitamin and mineral like this, and you will ultimately develop a personal supplement schedule.

In your workouts, you should constantly focus on further intensifying your training. Primarily, this will consist of gradually using heavier and heavier workout poundages. But there are also a number of intensification techniques you can use in your workouts. Here are five:

1. Go to failure on each set. This amounts to continuing a set until you literally can no longer finish a complete repetition of the movement you're using. On Bench Presses and Squats, be sure to have a spotter standing by when you train to failure.

2. Use the Weider *Forced Reps* training principle. This is a method in which you use a training partner to go even past the point of failure on an exercise. To do a set of forced reps, first go to failure and then have your training partner assist you in forcing out two or three more reps by pulling up on the weight just enough so you can complete each rep. Naturally, your muscles will fatigue so rapidly with forced reps that your partner will have to pull up much harder each rep than she did on the last one.

3. Use the Weider *Retro-Gravity* training principle. This principle consists of having two training partners lift a weight up for you, after which you *resist* the downward (negative) movement of the weight. Scientists have discovered that it's possible to gain as much strength and development from the negative phase of an exercise as from the positive (lifting) phase.

4. Use the Weider *Supersets* training principle. Supersets consist of two exercises done consecutively with no rest between them. Supersets are done either for antagonistic muscle groups (Bench Press + Bent Row = chest + back, or Leg Extension + Leg Curl = frontal thigh + thigh biceps), or within the same muscle group (Bench Press + Flyes = chest, or Pullovers + Bent Rowing = back).

5. Use the Weider *Quality Training* training principle. This consists of using the same weight, sets and reps for an exercise, but progressively reducing the rest time between sets. This training principle is usually used by bodybuilders just prior to competition, but quality training will drastically increase training intensity at any time.

ONWARD

In the next chapter, you will add to your pool of basic exercises by learning 24 intermediate and advanced exercises. Then these new movements will be combined into a wide variety of intermediate- and advanced-level training routines, tailored for virtually any goal you might have through weight training and bodybuilding.

5

Intermediate/Advanced Exercises and Routines

In this chapter we will expand on your pool of weight-training exercises by adding 24 new movements to your repertoire. As in Chapter 3, the exercises illustrated and explained in this chapter include movements using free weights, and Universal Gym and Nautilus machines.

At the end of this chapter, we will give you a final group of training programs, one or two of which you can use during your steady progression from intermediate to advanced bodybuilder or weight trainer.

POOL OF INTERMEDIATE/ADVANCED EXERCISES

Leg Raise

1. Emphasis—This movement stresses the frontal abdominal muscles, particularly the lower section. If you suffer from "tummy bulge" it would be a good idea to include Leg Raises in all of your workouts.

2. Starting Position—Lie on your back on the floor. Extend your arms above your head and grasp a heavy object (a chair, couch, etc.) to restrain your body during the movement. If you are on a special abdominal bench, you can grasp either the strap or the rollers at the top end of the bench. Bend your knees slightly, which will take potential strain off your lower back.

3. The Movement—Slowly raise your legs so your feet travel in a quarter circle from the floor or bench up to a point where they make a right angle with your torso. Lower slowly back to the starting point and repeat for the required number of repetitions.

4. Training Tip—You can give this movement a longer range of motion by lying back on a flat exercise bench with your hips at one end. Doing Leg Raises from this position allows you to lower your feet much further than when doing the movement on the floor or an abdominal bench.

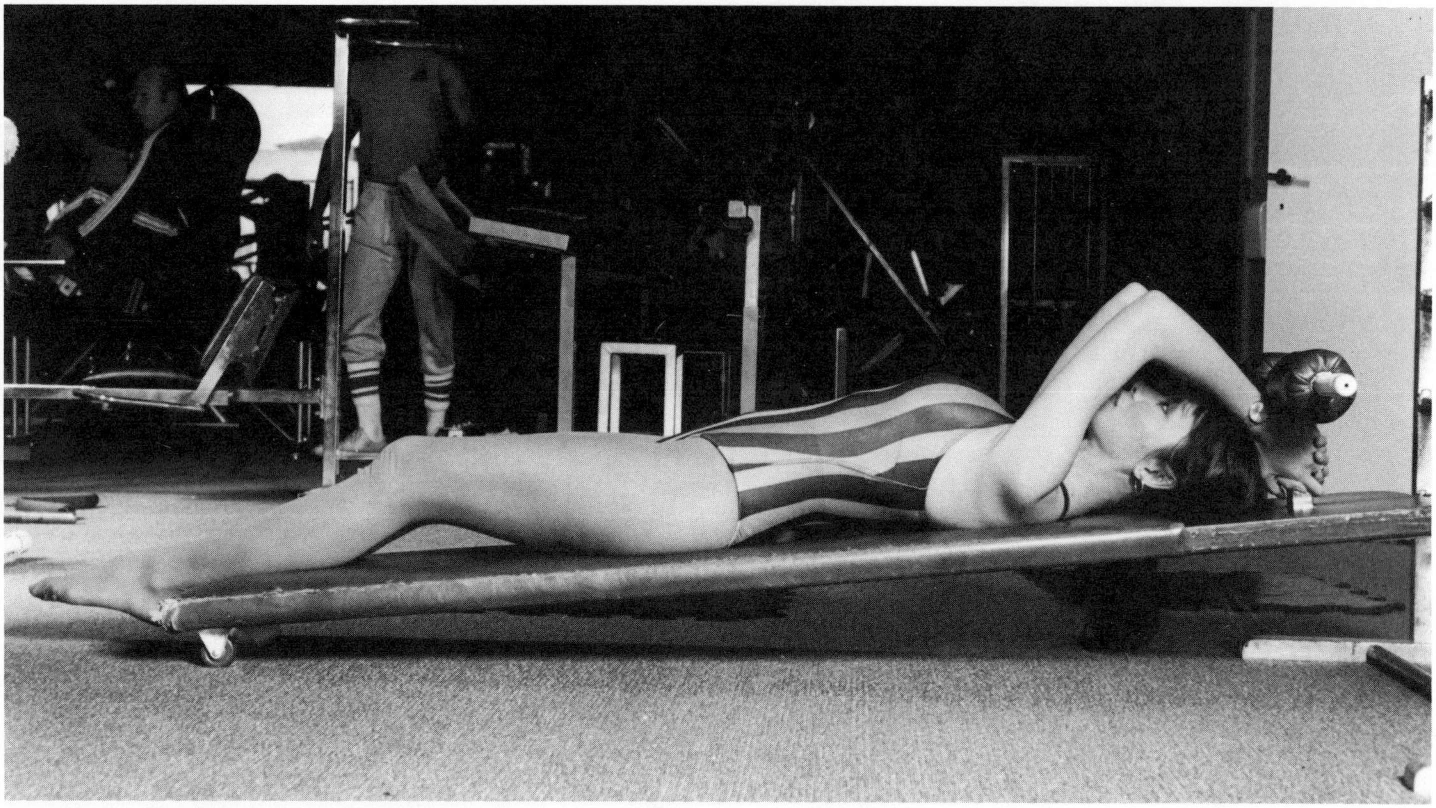

Leg Raise—start (above) and finish (below).

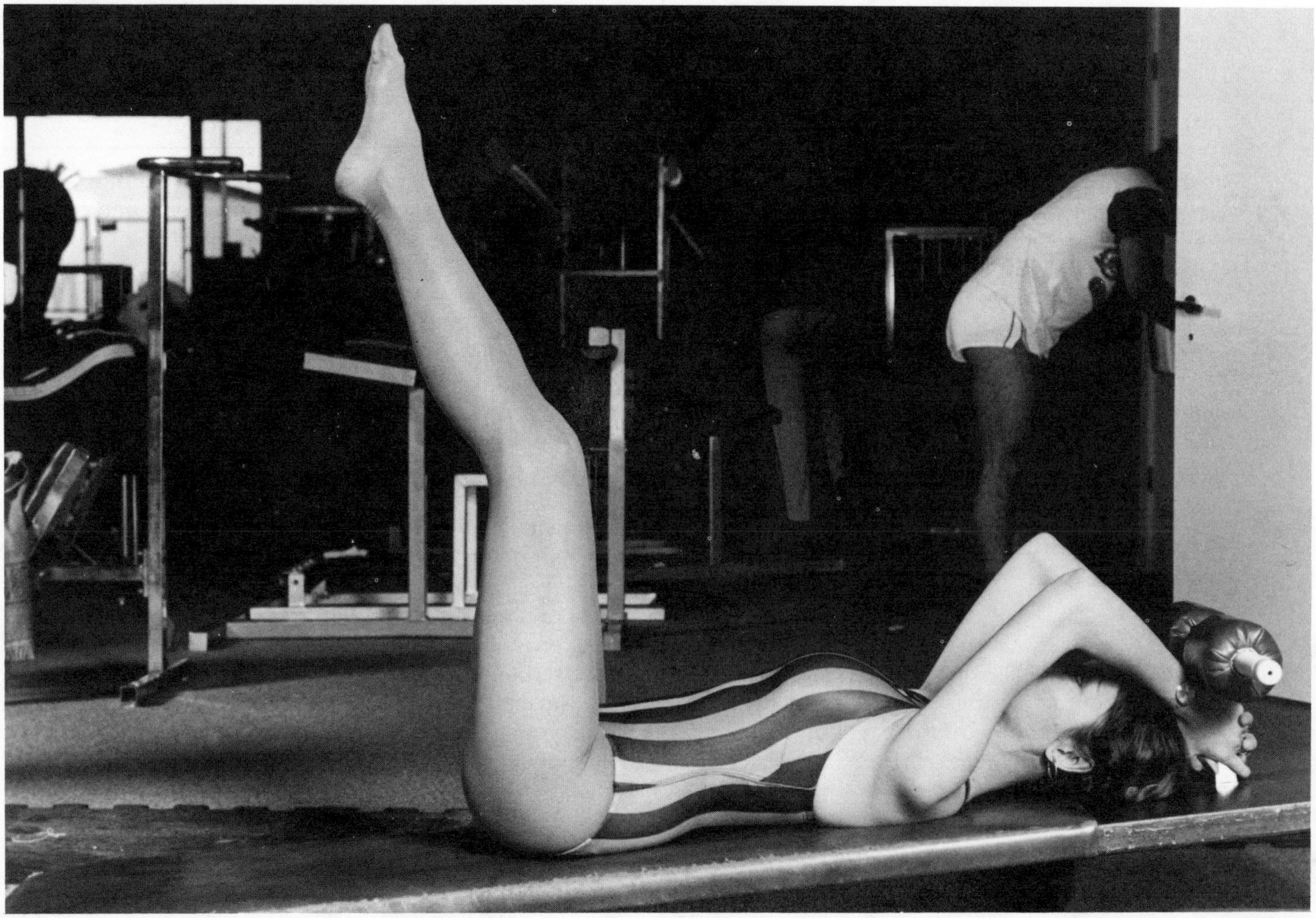

Seated Twisting

1. Emphasis—All twisting movements work the external oblique muscles on your side. This movement is quite popular with most women bodybuilders because it firms and tones the sides of their waists, giving their mid-sections a very trim appearance.

2. Starting Position—Sit on a flat exercise bench, and intertwine your legs in the upright legs of the bench. Place a broomstick or unloaded barbell behind your neck, and wrap your arms around the bar or stick.

3. The Movement—Twist your shoulders and torso as far as you can to the right. Then immediately twist as far as you can to the left. Repeat rhythmically from side to side, counting one full movement to both sides as a repetition. Repeat for the required number of repetitions.

4. Training Tip—Never use added resistance with the Seated Twisting movement. Your external obliques will grow in size rather rapidly if you use extra resistance, and any growth in muscle at the sides of your waist will make your waist look wider, not narrower.

Seated Twisting—start (and finish of one complete movement).

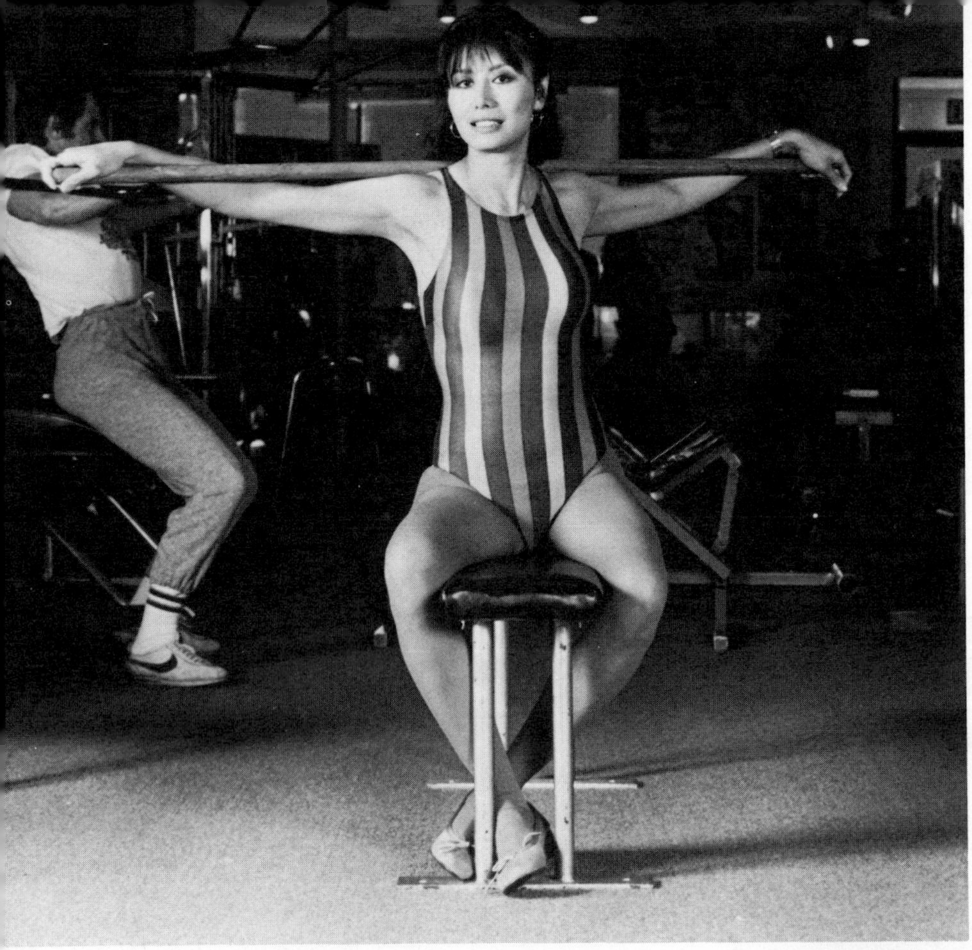

Seated Twisting—midpoint.

Seated Twisting—finish (and start of second half of one complete movement).

Seated Calf Machine

1. Emphasis—Doing Toe Raises with your knees bent at a right angle strongly stresses the broad soleus muscle, which lies under the gastrocnemius in your lower leg. The soleus gives width and curves to your calves.

2. Starting Position—Sit on the seat of the calf machine, and place your toes on the toe bar near the floor. Wedge your knees under the padded cross member at the top of the machine. Release the stop bar of the machine by pushing it forward. And finally, stretch your calf muscles by allowing your heels to sag downward as far below your toes as possible.

3. The Movement—Slowly extend your feet, and rise up on your toes as high as possible. Lower back to the stretched starting position, and repeat for the required number of repetitions.

4. Training Tips—As with all calf movements, be sure to use the three toe positions discussed with the calf exercises in Chapter 3. If you do not have a seated calf machine available, you can still do this movement with a barbell, a towel, and a 4 × 4-inch block of wood. Simply sit at the end of a bench with your toes on the block of wood. Wrap the towel around the middle of the handle of your barbell, which pads the bar and keeps it from digging into your knees when you place the weight on your thighs just above your knee caps. With the bar in this position, you can do the same movement as you would do on a seated calf machine.

Seated Calf Machine—start (left) and finish (right). Be sure to use three toe positions (in, straight forward, and out).

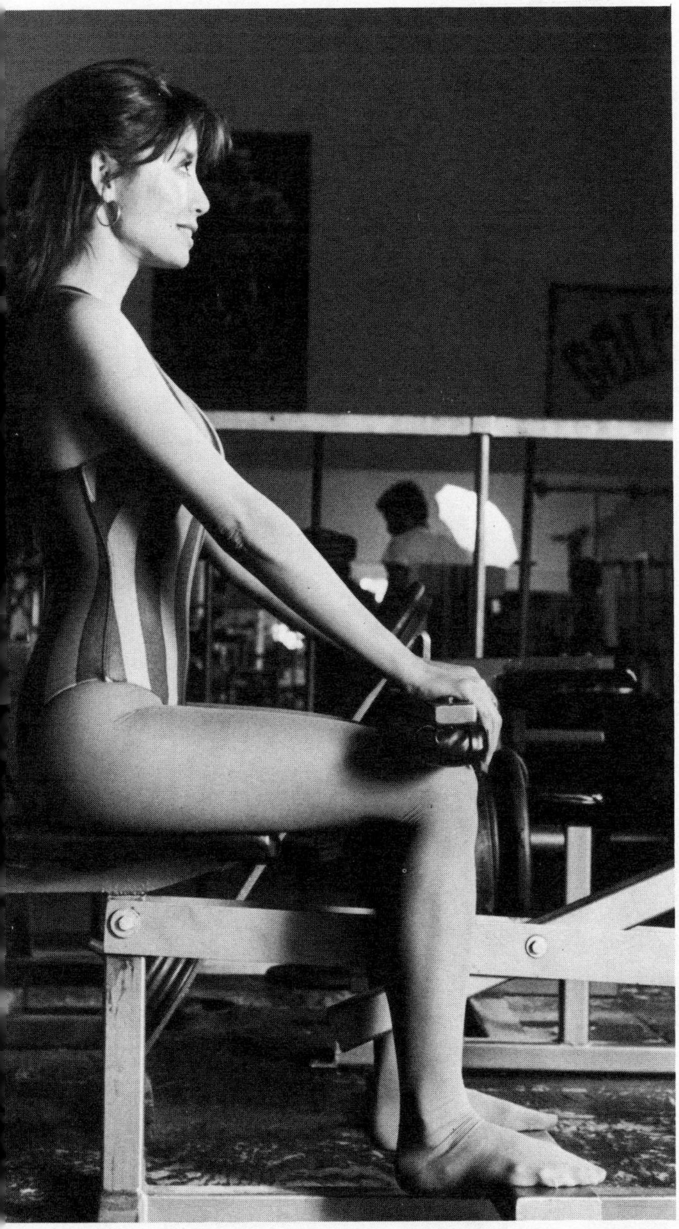

Calf Raise on Nautilus Omni Machine

1. Emphasis—This movement strongly stresses the gastrocnemius muscles on the backs of your lower legs. Secondary stress is placed on the soleus muscles.

2. Starting Position—Step into the hip belt that goes with the Nautilus omni machine, and pull the belt up around your waist. As you do this movement, the belt must be in a position where it bears the weight of the exercise across the top part of your hips and the lowest part of your spine. Attach the belt to the lever arm of the machine. Bend your legs and place the balls of your feet on one of the steps of the machine. Straighten your legs, and brace your upper body with your hands. Stretch your calves by allowing your heels to travel downward as far below your toes as possible.

3. The Movement—Rise up and down on your toes to the limit of your range of motion.

4. Training Tip—A very similar movement—called the Donkey Calf Raise—can be done with a heavy partner sitting astride your hips. Simply bend over until your torso is parallel to the floor, and place your hands on a flat exercise bench to support your body in this position. And, of course, you should place your toes on a block of wood to be sure you reach a full range of motion on the movement.

Calf Raise on Nautilus Omni Machine—start (left) and finish (right). Remember that the belt must be in a position where it bears the weight of the exercise across the top part of your hips and lowest part of your spine.

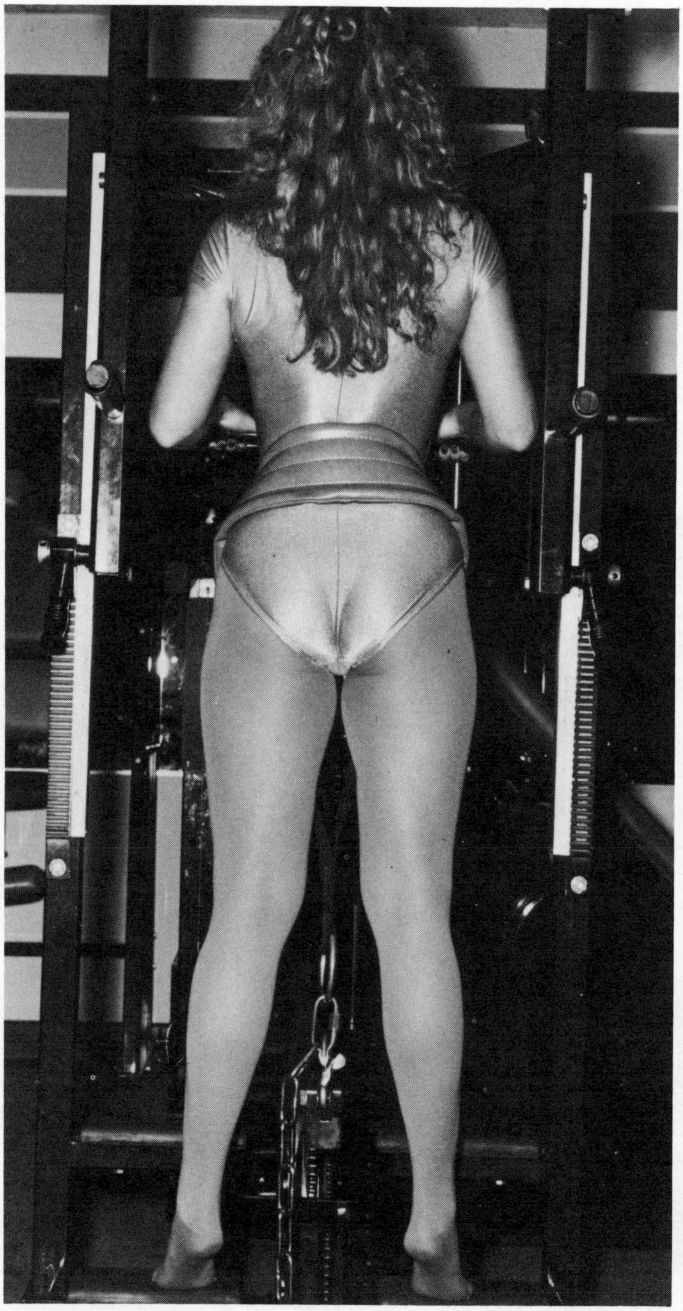

Hyperextension

1. **Emphasis**—This movement affects primarily the erector spinae muscles running up each side of your spine. Secondary emphasis is placed on the hamstring muscles at the backs of your thighs.

2. **Starting Position**—Stand in the middle of a Hyperextension bench, facing the surface of the machine that is padded on top. Hop upward and forward to place your pelvis on the machine's padded surface. You should be forward enough so that the upper part of your pelvis is at the front edge of the pad. Lean forward so your torso is hanging straight downward. As you do this, the backs of your calves will come to rest under the rear pads. They should remain there throughout the movement. Place your hands behind your head and keep them in that position for the balance of the movement.

3. **The Movement**—Straighten your back slowly, which will have the effect of moving your head in a quarter circle from hanging straight downward to facing directly ahead. Do not arch backward so far that your torso rises above an imaginary line drawn parallel to the floor. Return to the starting point, and repeat for the required number of repetitions.

4. **Training Tip**—If you don't have access to a Hyperextension bench, you can do this movement just as well by lying on a high table with your hips at the edge of the table. Simply have a training partner rest her torso across your calves to restrain your legs during the movement.

Hyperextension—start.

Hyperextension—finish.

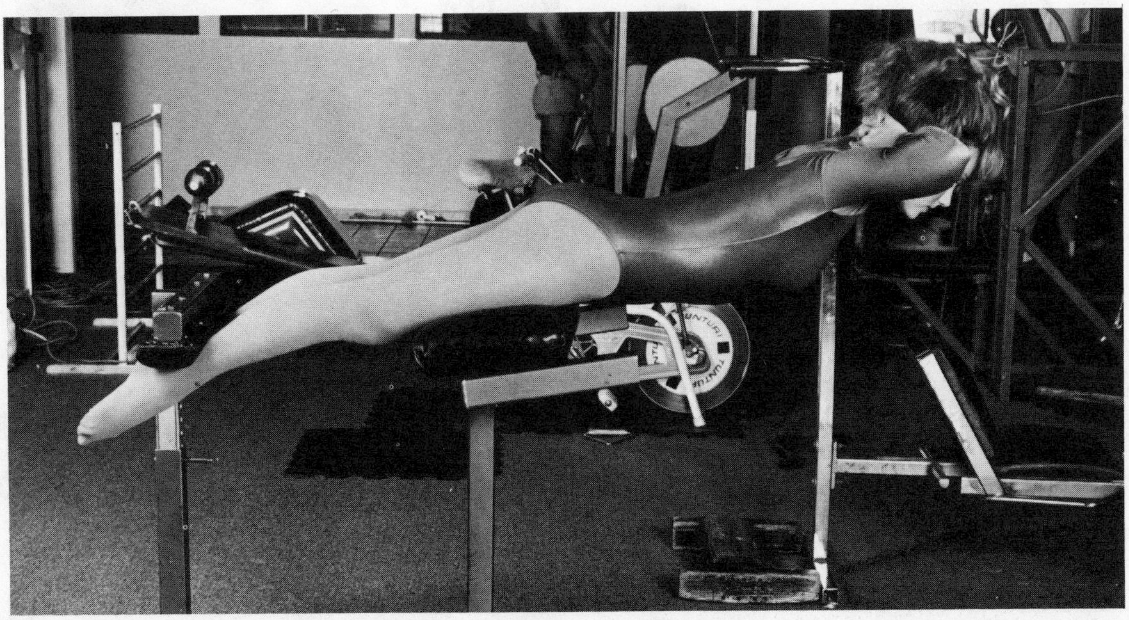

Deadlifts

1. Emphasis—This movement stresses all of the muscles of the back, particularly the erector spinae. It also places strong emphasis on the forearms and thighs.

2. Starting Position—Stand close to a barbell, your shins touching the bar. Bend your knees and back and grasp the bar with a shoulder-width grip, palms facing toward your shins. Your spine should be straight and at about a 45-degree angle with the floor. Your hips should be above your knees and your shoulders above your hips. Look straight ahead.

3. The Movement—Simultaneously straighten your legs and back to pull the barbell up to the tops of your thighs. (Keep your arms straight throughout the movement.) As soon as your body is completely straight, throw your shoulders back. Lower back to the starting position, and repeat for the required number of repetitions.

4. Training Tip—When using very heavy weights you might want to use a *reversed grip* (one palm facing forward, the other palm facing your body). This gives you a much more secure grip, since it prevents the bar from rolling out of your hands as you lift.

Deadlift—finish and start.

Nautilus Hip and Back Machine

1. Emphasis—This movement affects primarily the hip and lower back muscles. Secondary emphasis is placed on the hamstring muscles.

2. Starting Position—Lie on your back on the hip and back machine, with the backs of your knees against the roller pads and your hips as far away from the weight stack as possible. Fasten the lap belt around your hips. Grasp the machine's handles, and take resistance on the backs of your legs by forcing your knees down until your body is totally straight.

3. The Movement—Keeping your right leg straight, bend your left leg as much as possible, allowing your left knee to touch your torso at the bottom of the movement. Push your left leg back to the starting position and repeat the movement with your right leg. Alternate legs for the required number of repetitions.

4. Training Tip—Of all the machines that Nautilus puts out, this is the only one that can firm and tone your hips and upper thighs.

Nautilus Hip and Back Machine—start and finish (left), and midpoint for right leg (right).

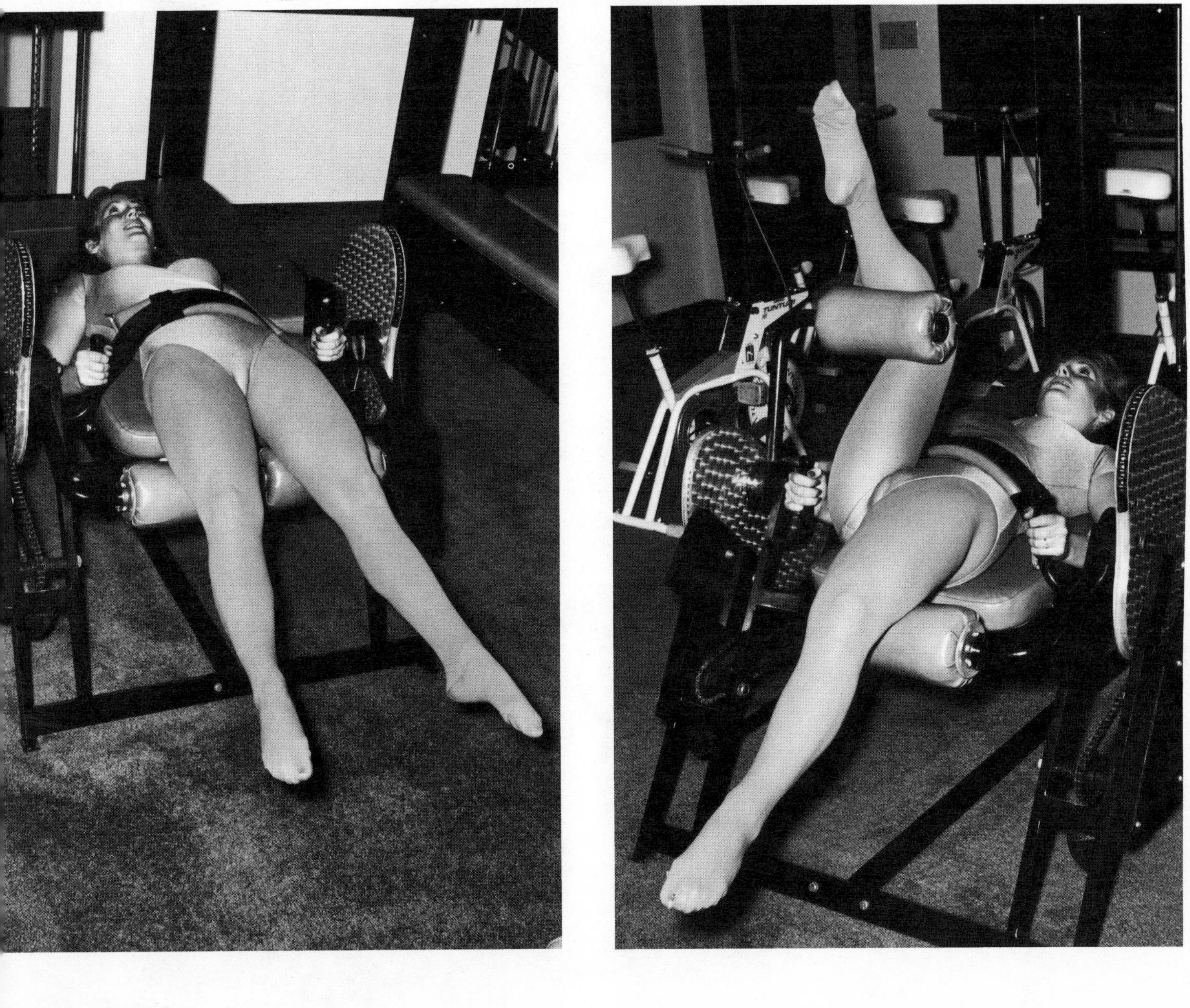

Upright Rowing

1. Emphasis—Upright Rowing stresses the shoulder muscles and trapezius muscles of the upper back. This is a particularly fine exercise for promoting good posture.

2. Starting Position—Grasp a barbell or the handle of the floor pulley on a Universal Gym with a narrow grip (six inches between your index fingers). Your palms should be toward your body. Stand erect with your arms hanging straight down and the barbell or pulley handle resting across your upper thighs.

3. The Movement—Keeping the barbell or pulley handle close to your body, pull it slowly up to your chin, emphasizing an upward movement with your shoulders. At the top of the movement, your elbows should be higher than your hands, and your shoulders should be rolled back. Lower slowly back to the starting position, and repeat for the required number of repetitions.

4. Training Tip—In all movements (and particularly the Upright Rowing exercise), it is essential to lower the weight slowly. You can actually build as much strength and muscle tone on the downward half of a movement as on the upward half.

Upright Rowing—finish and start.

Shrugs—finish and start.

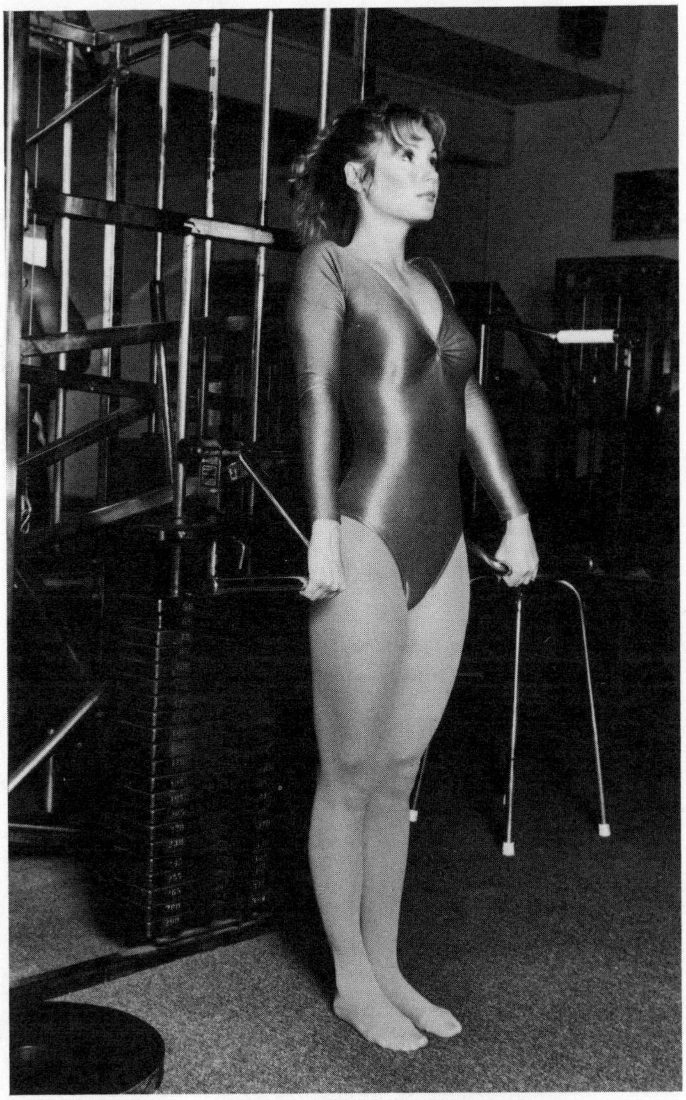

Shrug (finish) using Universal Gym bench press station.

Shrugs

1. Emphasis—This movement affects the powerful trapezius muscles of your upper back. Shrugs are an excellent movement for promoting good body posture.

2. Starting Position—Using a barbell, stand erect with the barbell in your hands, palms facing your body and your hands set at shoulder width. With two dumbbells, hold the bells across the tops of your thighs. At the Bench Press station of a Universal Gym, face the weight stack and grasp the handles of the machine with your palms facing your body. (If you are too short to allow yourself to have resistance on your hands when you are standing erect, you will have to stand on a block of wood to raise your shoulders a few inches higher.) On a Nautilus machine, sit on the seat and force your forearms between the pads, palms facing downward. With all variations of the movement, relax your trapezius muscles, and allow your shoulders to sag downward as far as possible at the starting position.

3. The Movement—On all variations of the Shrug, simply shrug your shoulders upward and backward as high as you can, almost trying to touch the points of your shoulders to your ears. Lower back to the starting position, and repeat for the required number of repetitions.

4. Training Tip—Using dumbbells for Shrugs allows you to have the longest range of motion.

Seated Pulley Rowing

1. **Emphasis**—Of all back movements, Seated Pulley Rows give the most thorough stimulation to all parts of the back—the latissimus dorsi, erector spinae, and trapezius. Secondary stimulation is provided to the biceps and forearm muscles.

2. **Starting Position**—With a Universal Gym floor pulley, grasp the handle with your palms facing downward and your index fingers about six to eight inches apart. Sit on the floor facing the pulley. On a free-weight floor pulley, grasp the handle as you would on a Universal Gym, brace your feet on the foot bar, and sit down in the apparatus. With both variations, lean forward and straighten your arms fully at the start of the movement.

3. **The Movement**—Simultaneously sit erect and pull your hands toward your body to touch at the bottom edge of your rib cage. As you pull the handle toward your body, be sure to keep your elbows in close to the sides of your torso. Return to the starting position, and repeat for the required number of repetitions.

4. **Training Tip**—If you have access to a pulley handle with parallel gripping surfaces, you will find that you can isolate your arms from the movement more with this handle than with a standard bar handle.

Seated Pulley Row—start, as seen from front.

Seated Pulley Row—start, as seen from behind (above), and finish (below). Be sure to keep elbows in close to your sides.

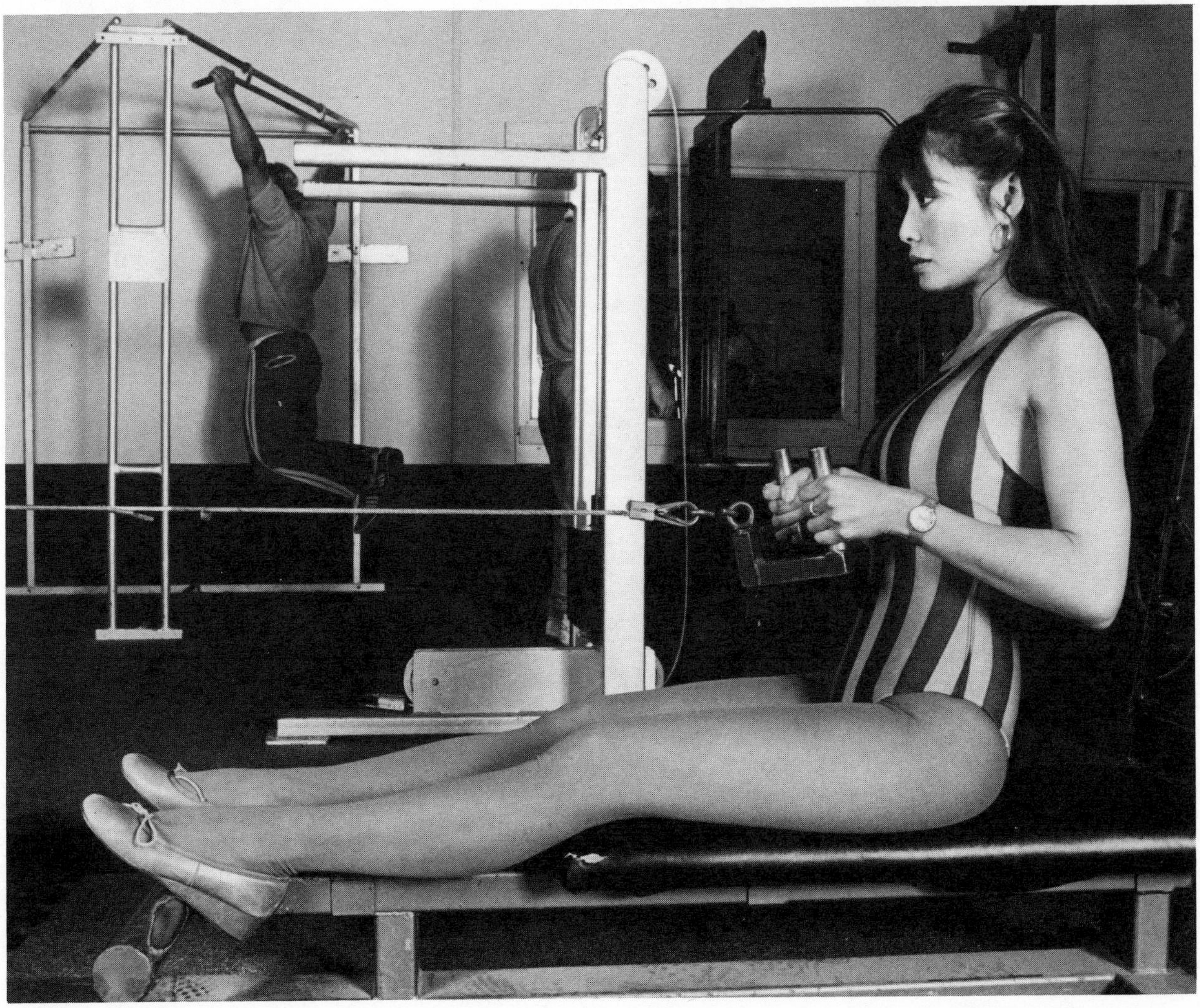

Nautilus Rowing Machine—start.

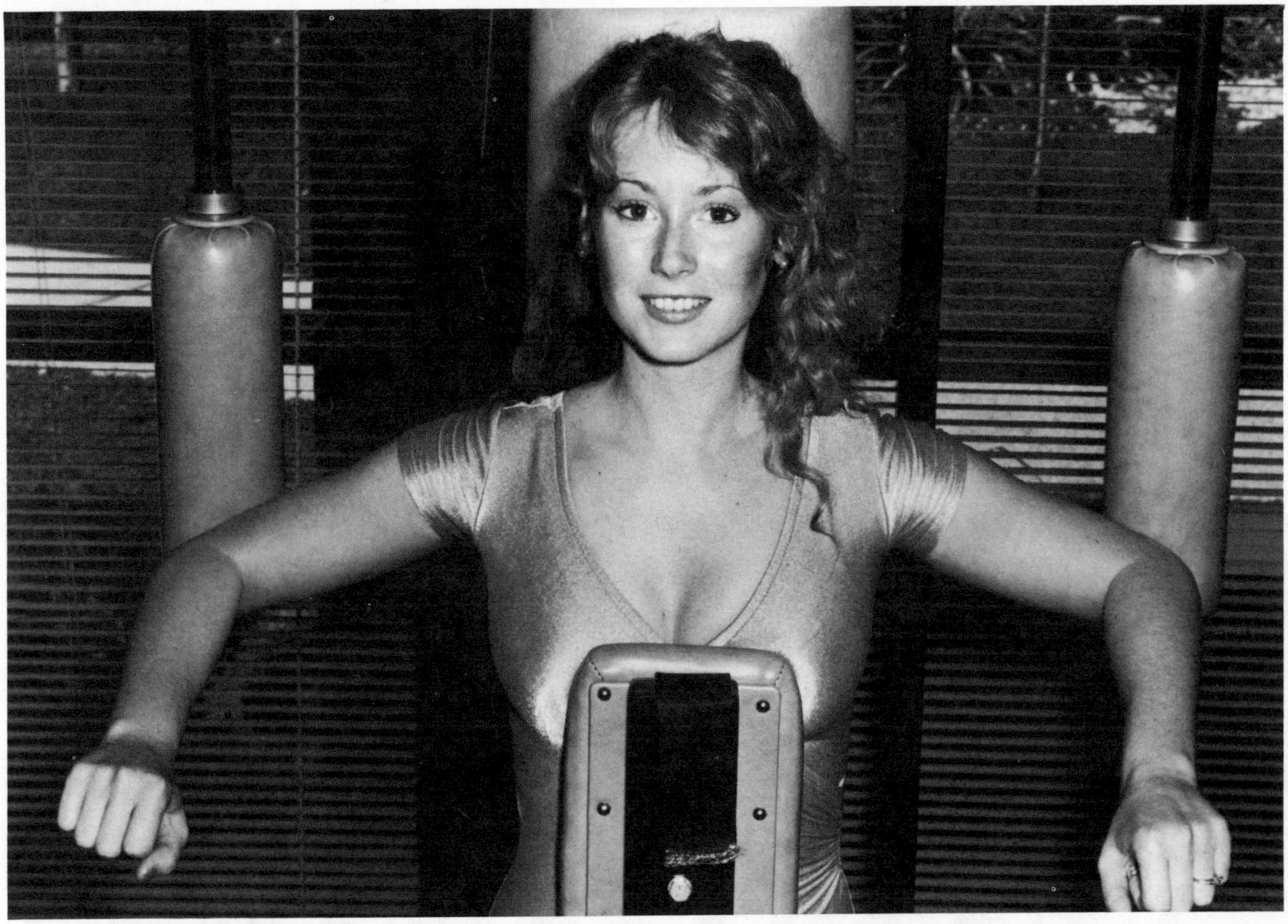

Nautilus Rowing Machine—finish. Shifting the position of your forearms will shift emphasis on muscle groups: forearms parallel to floor—latissimus dorsi muscles; forearms perpendicular to floor—posterior deltoid muscles.

Nautilus Rowing Machine

1. Emphasis—This movement stresses the latissimus dorsi muscles of your upper back, with secondary emphasis placed on your trapezius and the posterior heads of your deltoids.

2. Starting Position—Sit in the machine facing away from the weight stack. Place your arms between the vertical roller pads so the backs of your upper arms rest against the inner edges of the pads.

3. The Movement—Slowly force your upper arms directly backward as far as possible, moving the roller pads in semicircles to the rear. Pause for a count of two in this contracted position, and lower back to the starting point. Repeat for the required number of repetitions.

4. Training Tips—If you keep your forearms parallel to the floor during this movement, you will place major stress on your latissimus dorsi muscles. But if you keep your forearms perpendicular to the floor during the movement, stress is shifted more to your posterior deltoid muscles.

Dumbbell Bent Rowing

1. Emphasis—As with a Barbell Bent Rowing movement, this exercise stresses all of the back muscles, particularly the latissimus dorsi. Secondary stress is placed on the biceps and forearms.

2. Starting Position—Bend over at the waist until your torso is parallel to the floor. Unlock your legs slightly to take strain off your lower back during the movement. Grasp two dumbbells, and let them hang at arms' length directly below your chest.

3. The Movement—Being sure that your upper arm bones travel out toward the sides, pull the dumbbells up until they touch your chest. Lower back to the starting position, and repeat for the required number of repetitions.

4. Training Tip—This movement is often done one arm at a time. In this case you should brace your body with your free hand resting on a flat exercise bench. To be sure that you get a full stretch in your latissimus dorsi at the start of each repetition, place the foot on the same side as your exercising arm backward and your other foot forward for the movement.

Dumbbell Bent Rowing—start and finish.

Dumbbell Bent Rowing—one-arm variation.

Leg Extensions

1. Emphasis—This mc.ement places very direct stress on the quadriceps muscles on the fronts of your thighs.

2. Starting Position—This exercise can be done on a free-weight machine, a Nautilus machine, or a Universal Gym machine. In all variations, sit at the edge of the bench or seat, and hook your insteps under the lower roller pads. Grasp the handles that are provided or the edges of the bench to steady your body in position during the movement.

3. The Movement—Slowly straighten your legs. Pause at the top of the movement for a count of two and lower back to the starting point. Repeat for the required number of repetitions.

4. Training Tip—You can do this movement one leg at a time if you wish. On all one-leg and one-arm exercises you will find that you can concentrate much harder on the movement than when using both arms or both legs at the same time.

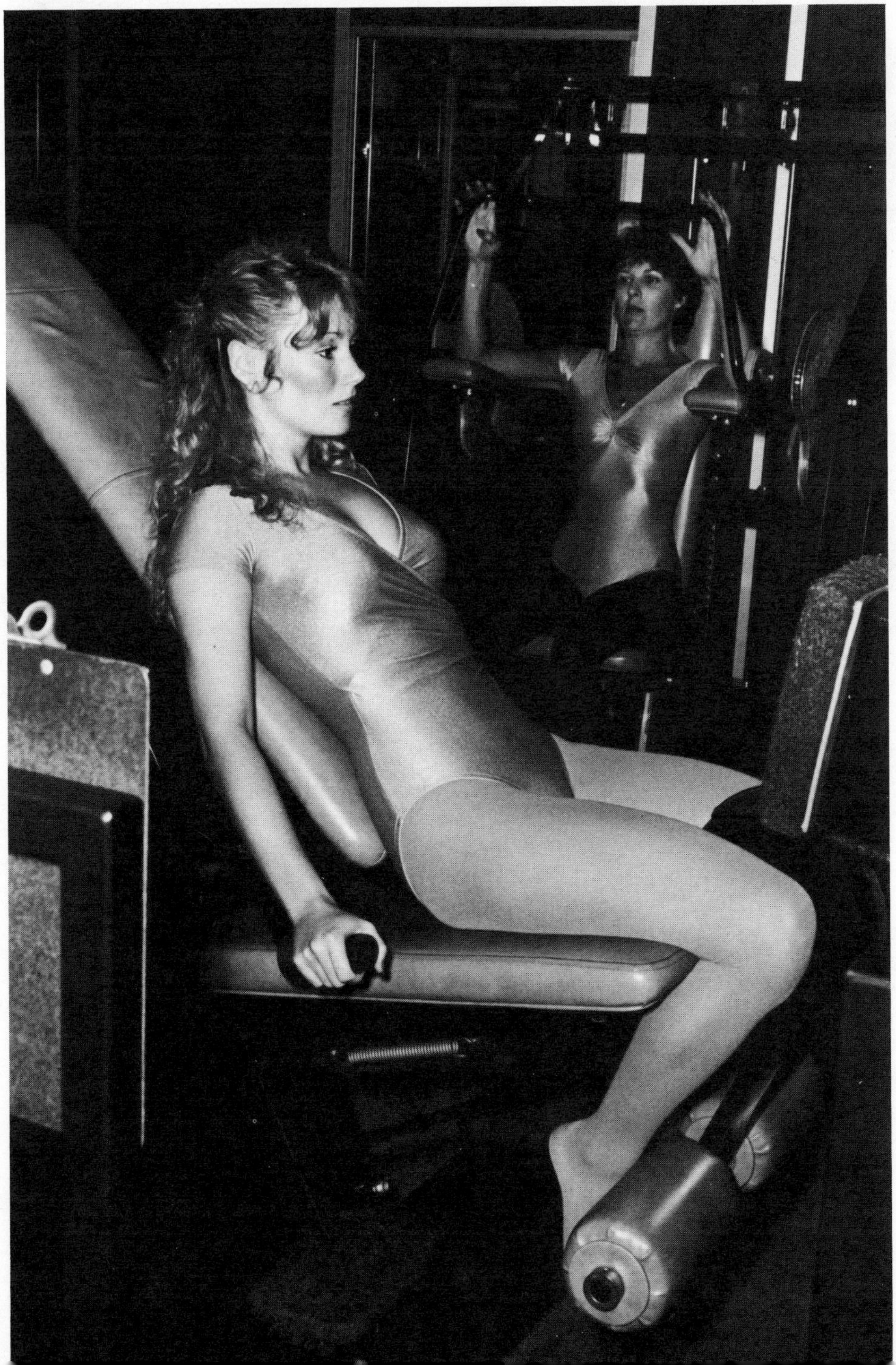

Leg Extension on Nautilus machine—start.

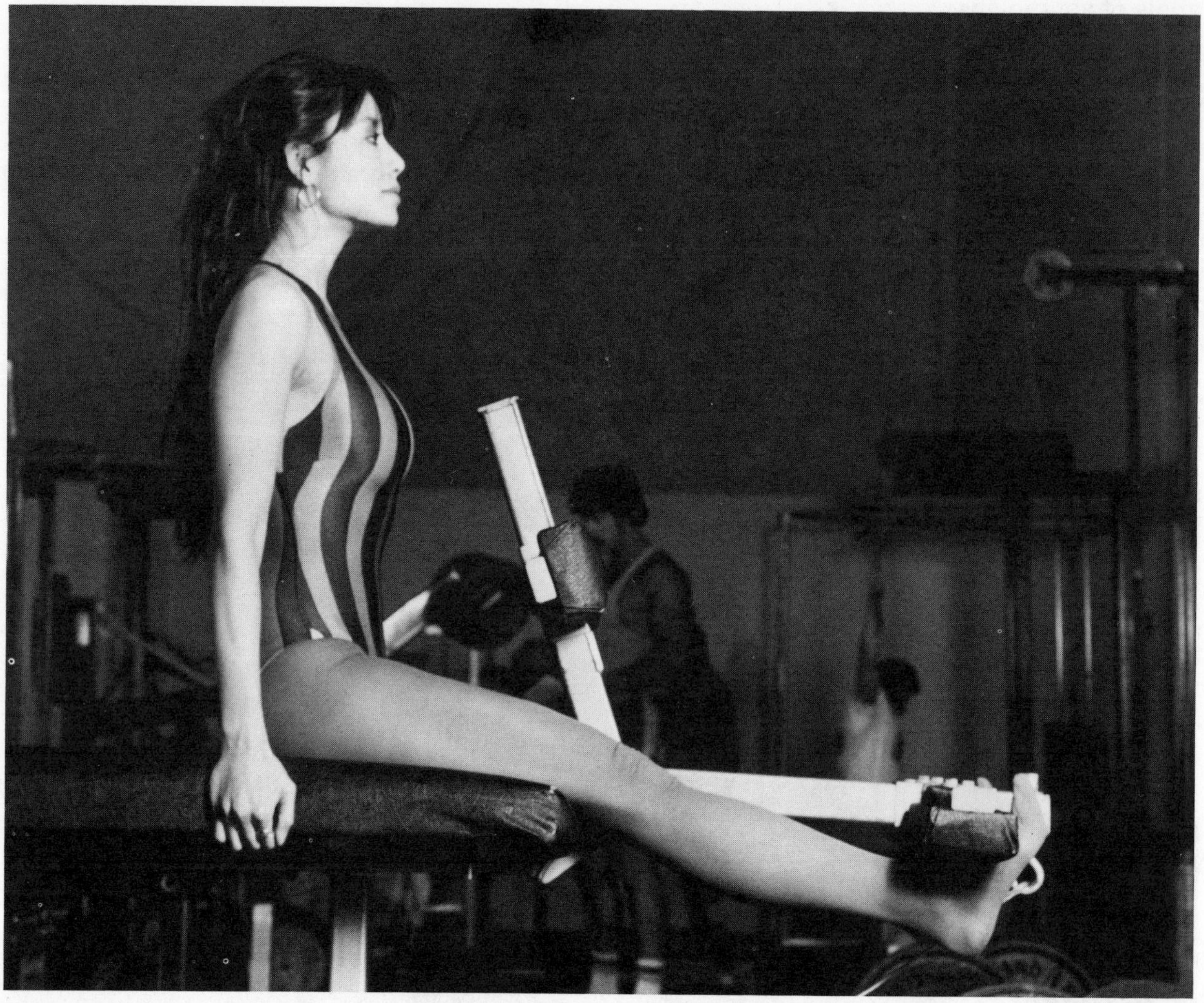

Leg Extension on free-weight machine—finish. This movement also can be done one leg at a time.

Leg Curls

1. Emphasis—This exercise places direct stress on the biceps femoris (hamstring) muscles at the backs of your thighs.

2. Starting Position—As with Leg Extensions, this movement can be done on a free-weight machine, a Nautilus machine, or a Universal Gym machine. On all three machines lie face down with your knees at the edge of the padded table. Hook your heels under the roller pads. Grasp the handles provided or the sides of the table to steady your body in position during the exercise.

3. The Movement—Slowly bend your legs to the full extent of their range of motion. Pause for a count of two at the top of the movement, and lower back to the starting point. Repeat for the required number of repetitions.

4. Training Tip—Be sure that you keep your hips in contact with the bench at all times during this movement. There is a tendency to allow your hips to come up off the bench during Leg Curls. But this is cheating and it only robs you of part of the exercise's range of motion.

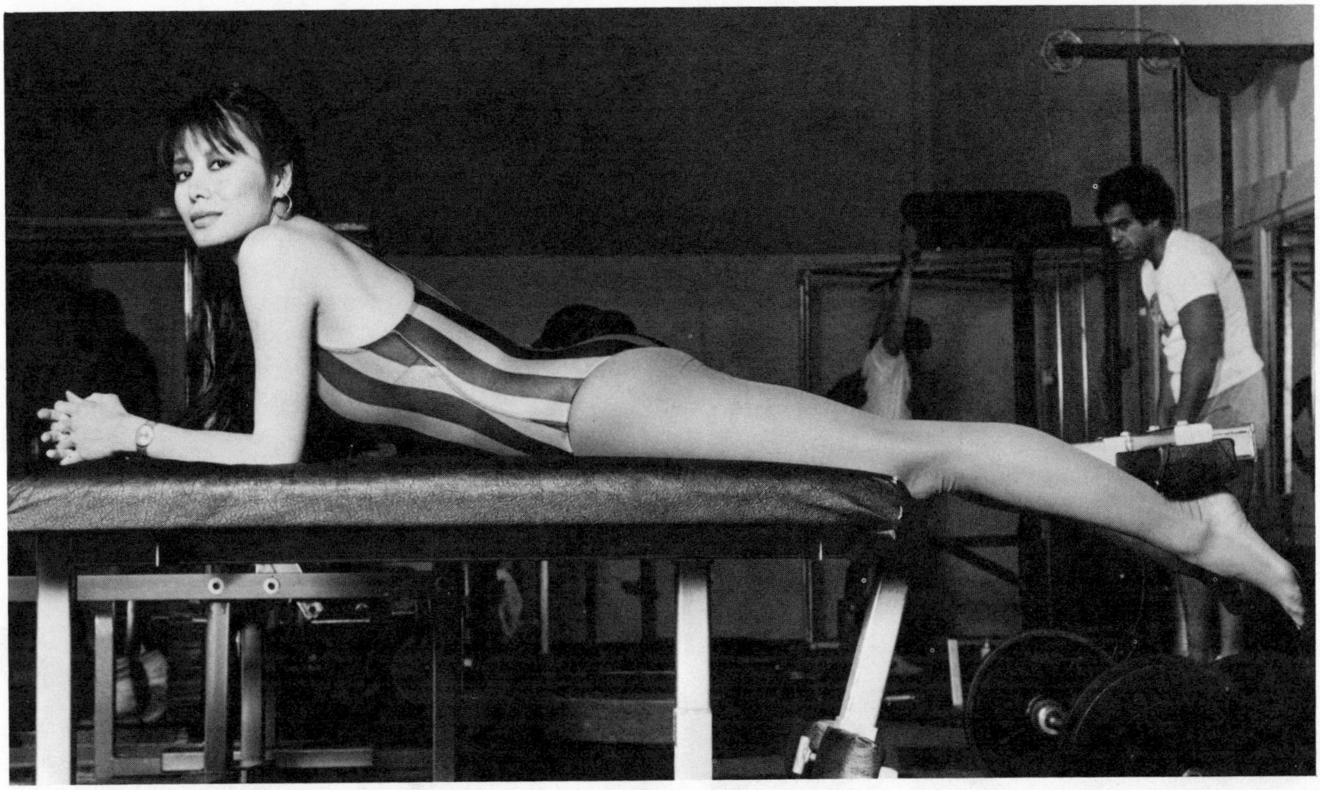

Leg Curl—start on free-weight machine (above), and finish on Nautilus machine (below).

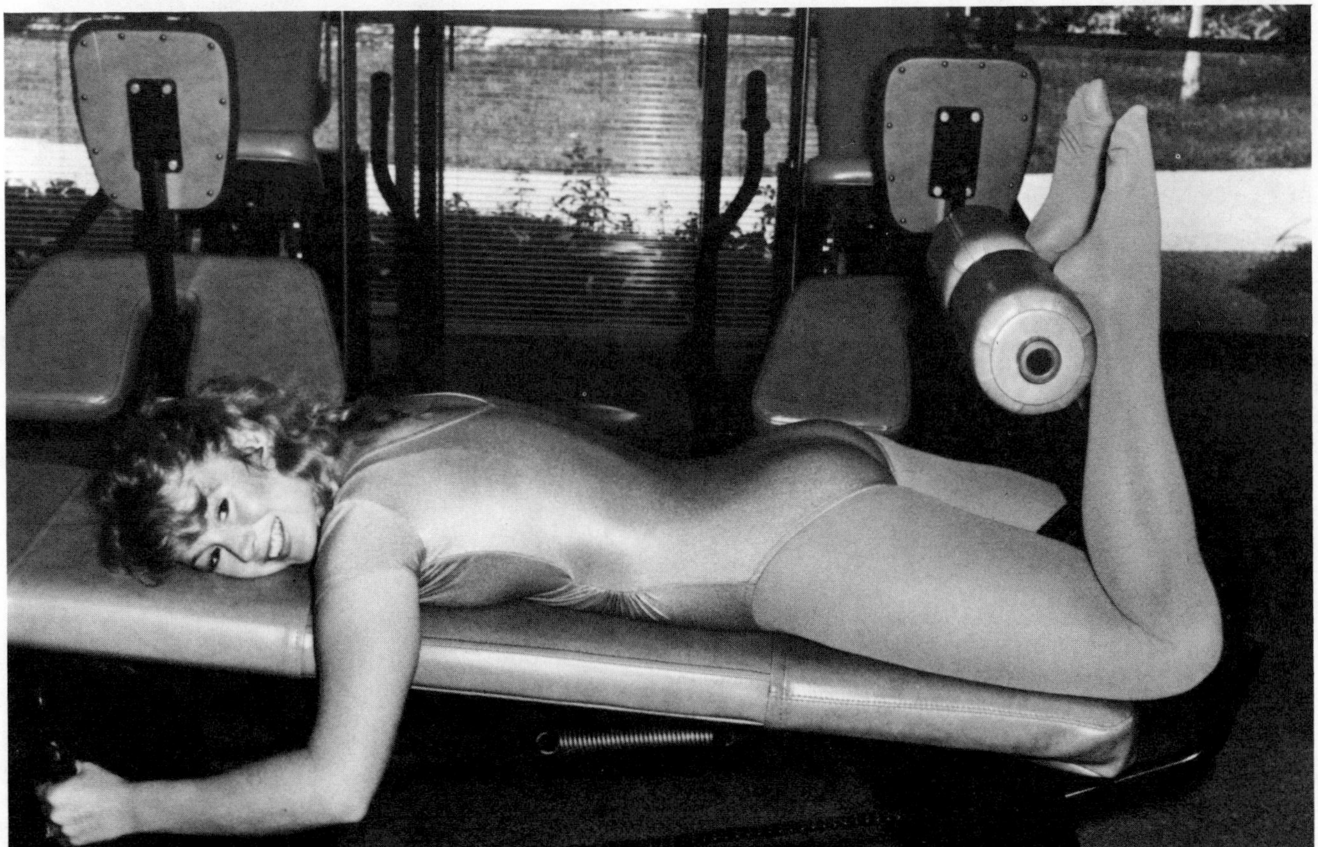

Incline Press

1. Emphasis—By doing barbell, dumbbell, or Universal Gym presses on an incline bench, you stress the upper part of your pectorals, your frontal deltoids, and your triceps.

2. Starting Position—Using a barbell or two dumbbells in your hands, lie back on a 45-degree incline bench, and extend your arms so they are perpendicular to the floor and the dumbbells or barbell are directly above your chest. At the Universal Gym Seated Press station lie back on the incline bench, grasp the handles of the pressing apparatus, and extend your arms.

3. The Movement—On all variations, lower the weight(s) directly downward until it touches your chest. Be sure that your upper arm bones travel directly out to the sides as you lower and raise the weights. Push back to the starting position, and repeat for the required number of repetitions.

4. Training Tip—You will achieve the greatest range of movement with dumbbells, because they can be lowered well below your shoulders, while a barbell would contact your chest and terminate the movement long before your hands could reach their lowest possible position.

Incline Press with barbell—start.

Incline Press with dumbbells—finish (right).

Flyes

1. Emphasis—This movement stresses primarily the pectoral muscles with secondary emphasis placed on the deltoids. When Flyes are done on an incline bench, stress is placed primarily on the upper part of the pectorals, while on a decline bench stress is shifted to the lower pectorals. When done on a flat bench, Flyes hit both parts of the pectoral muscles.

2. Starting Position—Lie back on a flat, incline, or decline bench with two dumbbells held in your hands. Extend your arms so they are perpendicular to the floor. Bend your elbows slightly.

3. The Movement—Keeping your elbows slightly bent, lower the dumbbells in semicircles out to the sides to the full extent of your pectorals' range of motion. Return along the same arc to the starting position, and repeat for the required number of repetitions.

4. Training Tip—Keep your palms facing upward throughout the movement.

Flyes on flat bench—start.

Flyes on flat bench—finish (above).

Flyes on incline bench—finish (below).

Side Laterals

1. Emphasis—This movement stresses the deltoid muscles, particularly the medial heads of the deltoids. Secondary stress is placed on the trapezius muscles.

2. Starting Position—With two dumbbells in your hands, stand erect with the bells resting on the tops of your thighs. Your arms should be slightly bent at the start of the movement. On a Nautilus machine, adjust the seat until you can sit in it with your shoulders on the same level as the pivot point of the machine's cams. Fasten the seat belt, and place the backs of your wrists against the pads at the ends of the movement arms.

3. The Movement—In both variations, slowly raise your arms out to the sides until they reach the level of an imaginary line drawn parallel to the floor. Pause for a moment at the top of the movement, and then lower back to the starting position. Repeat for the required number of repetitions.

4. Training Tip—With dumbbells there is a tendency to swing the weight up. This happens primarily when you do the movement with an overly quick cadence. So be sure to move the weights slowly, and *feel* the resistance in your deltoids.

Side Laterals—start (left) and finish (right).

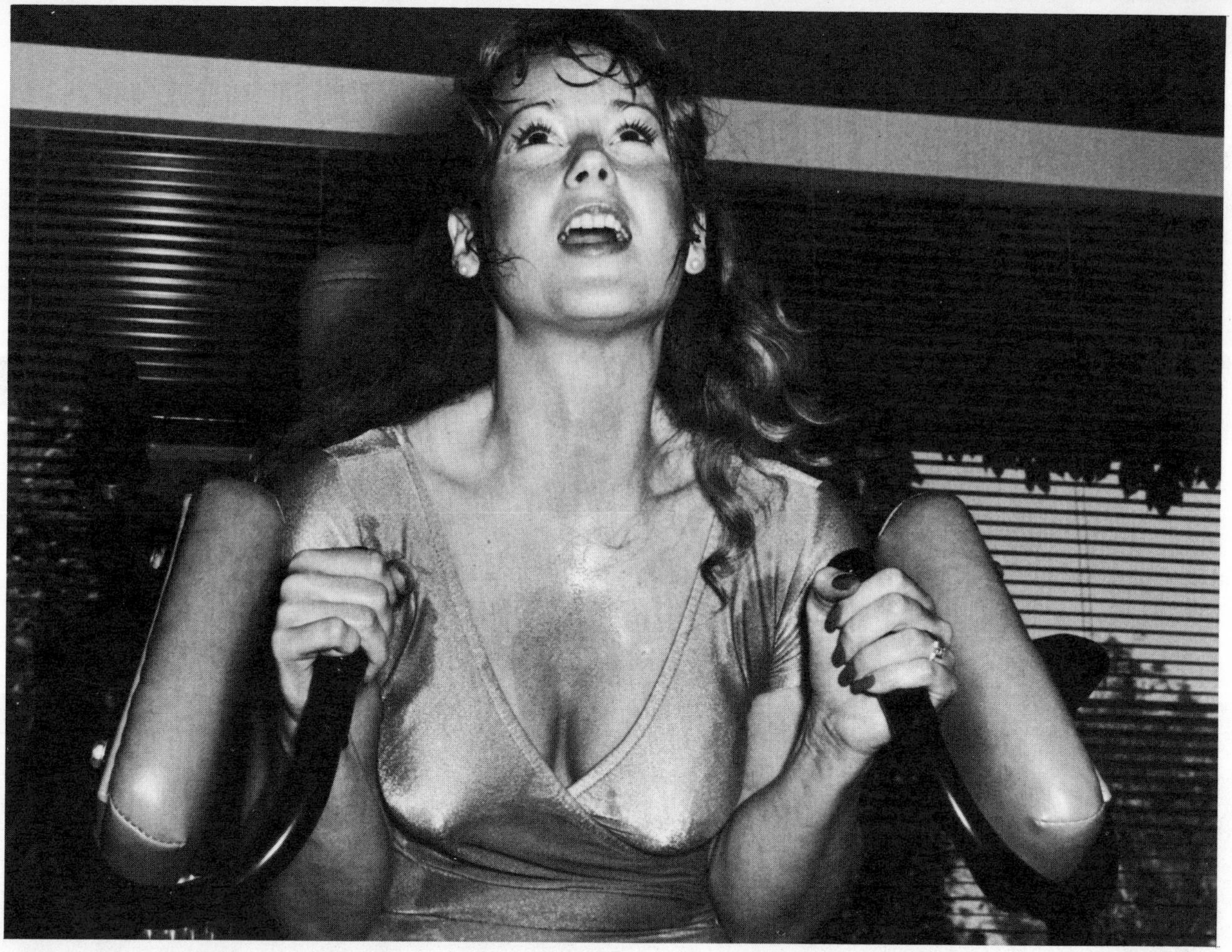

Side Laterals on Nautilus machine—start (above) and *midpoint* (below). Continue movement of arms until they are straight out to sides and parallel to floor.

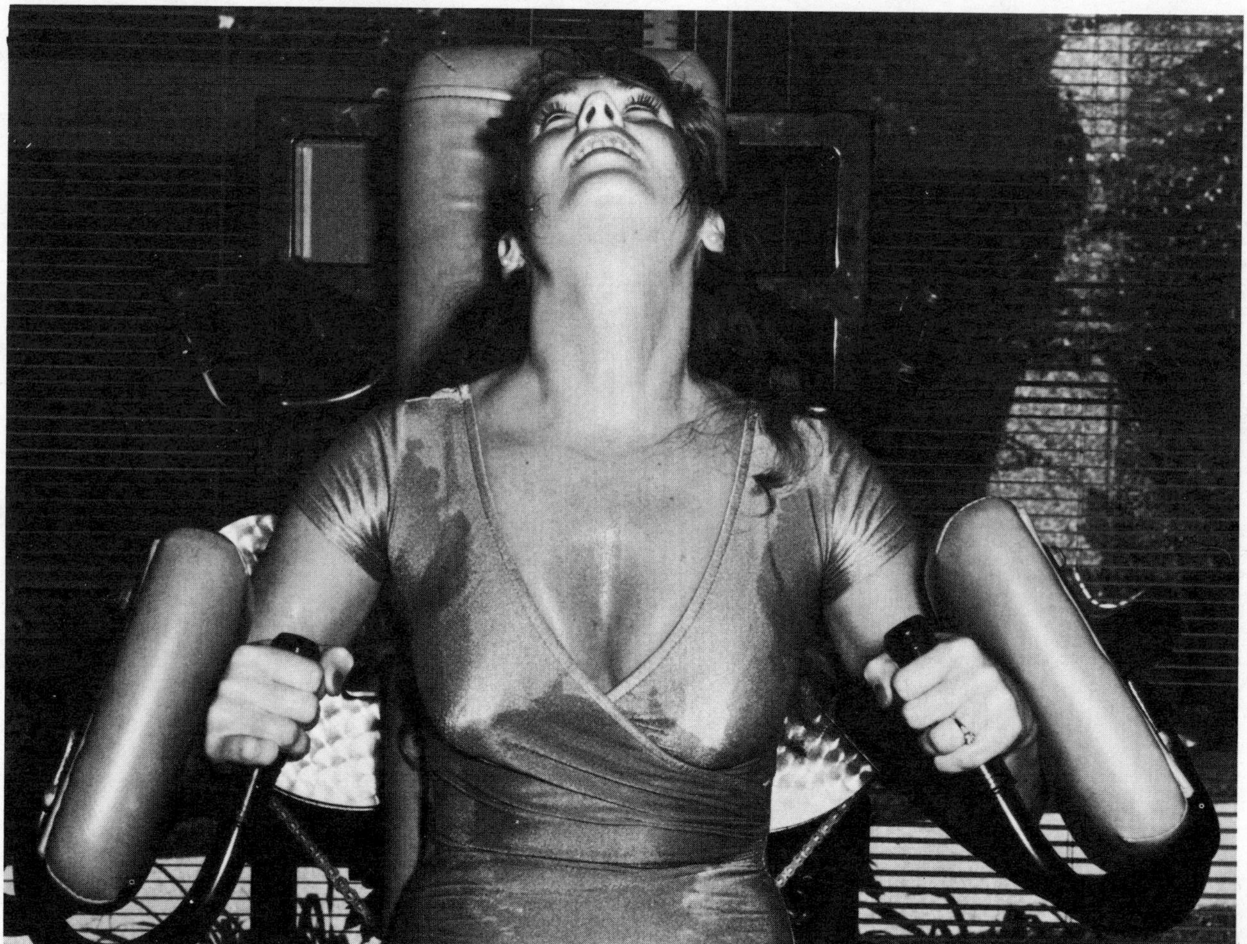

Press Behind the Neck

1. Emphasis—This movement stresses the deltoids—particularly the anterior heads—triceps and trapezius muscles.

2. Starting Position—Grasp a barbell with a grip about three to four inches wider on each side than shoulder width. Stand erect with the barbell resting on your trapezius behind your neck.

3. The Movement—Keeping your elbows under the bar at all times, press the weight directly upward to arms' length. Lower back to the starting point and repeat.

4. Training Tip—You can also do this movement seated at the end of a flat exercise bench, which isolates your legs from the exercise. You will find that you cannot use as much weight seated as standing when doing Presses Behind the Neck.

Press Behind the Neck—start and finish.

Dumbbell Press

1. Emphasis—Like Presses Behind the Neck, this movement stresses the deltoids—particularly the anterior heads—triceps, and trapezius muscles.

2. Starting Position—Stand erect and pull two dumbbells to your shoulders, so that your palms are facing forward.

3. The Movement—Slowly push the dumbbells directly upward from your shoulders until your arms are locked out straight and the dumbbells are directly above your head. Lower slowly back to the starting point, and repeat for the required number of repetitions.

4. Training Tip—This movement can be done with alternate arms. Simply push one dumbbell completely up. Then as that dumbbell begins to come back down, slowly push the other one up to arms' length. Repeat in alternate fashion for the required number of repetitions.

Dumbbell Press—start and finish (left) and alternating arms (right).

Incline Dumbbell Curls

1. Emphasis—This movement places strong emphasis on the biceps muscles. Secondary stress is placed on the forearm muscles.

2. Starting Position—Lie back on a 45-degree incline bench. You should have two dumbbells in your hands, and your arms should be dangling straight downward. Your palms should be facing directly forward.

3. The Movement—Keeping your upper arms motionless, curl the dumbbells in semicircles directly forward until they reach shoulder height. Lower the dumbbells back to the starting point, and repeat for the required number of repetitions.

4. Training Tip—By curling the dumbbells slightly out to the sides instead of directly forward, you can put an entirely different type of stress on your biceps muscles.

Incline Dumbbell Curl—start (left) and finish (right).

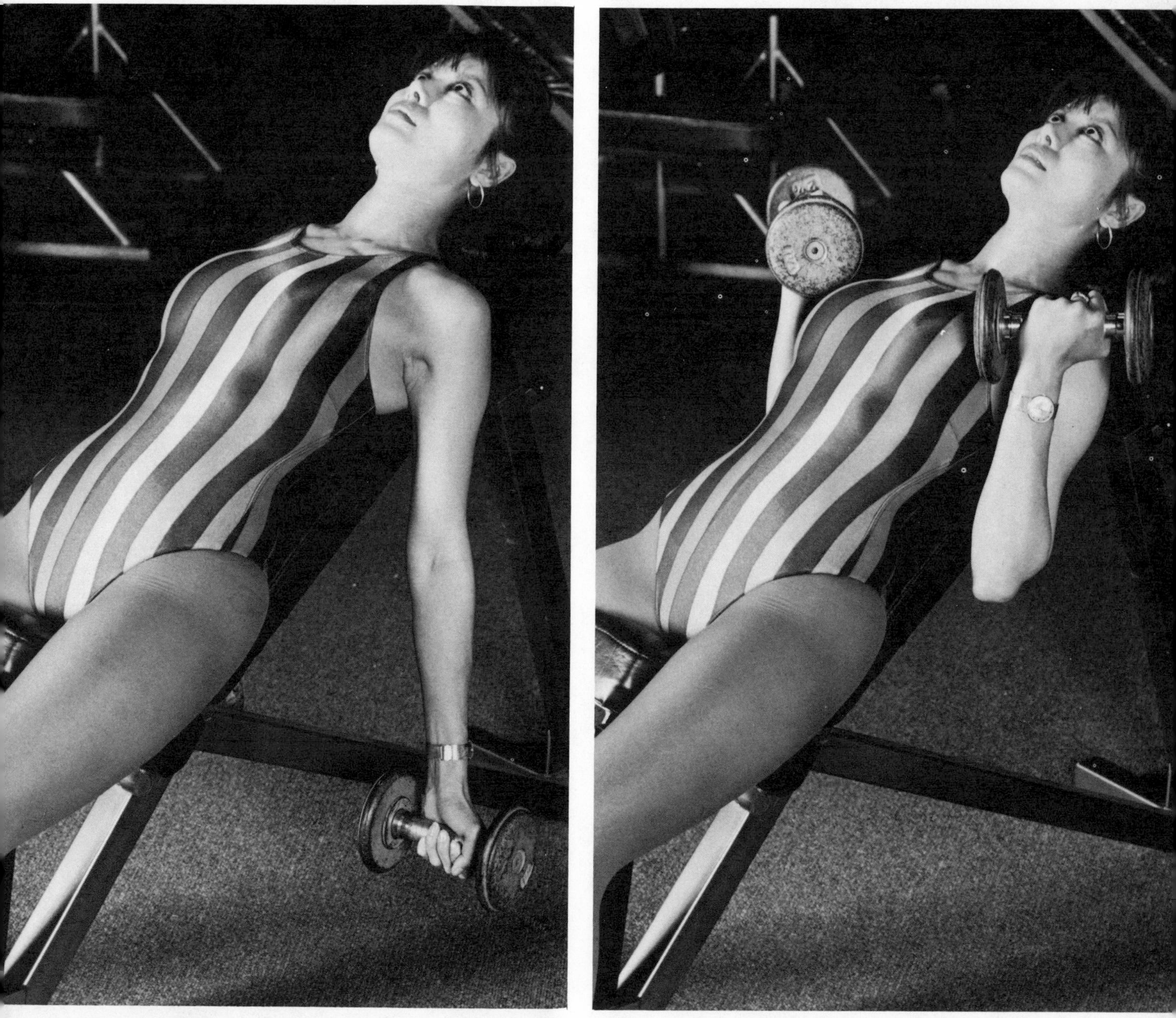

Concentration Curls

1. Emphasis—Concentration curls primarily affect the biceps muscle, while placing secondary emphasis on the muscles of the forearms.

2. Starting Position—Sit at the end of a flat exercise bench. Take a dumbbell in one hand and bend forward enough so you can place the elbow of that arm against the inside of your thigh near your knee. Place your free hand on the same thigh so the forearm of your free hand braces the elbow of your exercising arm.

3. The Movement—From this starting position, slowly curl the dumbbell up as high as you can. Lower back to the starting point, and repeat for the required number of repetitions.

4. Training Tip—Concentration Curls are also occasionally done by running the upper arm down the top edge of an incline bench, which restrains your upper arm as you curl up the dumbbell.

Concentration Curl—start (above).

Concentration Curl—finish (right).

Standing Triceps Extension

1. Emphasis—This movement puts a strong stress on the triceps muscles and puts secondary emphasis on the muscles of the forearms.

2. Starting Position—Take a narrow grip (six inches between your index fingers) in the middle of a barbell, and swing the weight up to the finish position for a Military Press. Press your upper arms against the side of your head and keep them in this position for the entire movement.

3. The Movement—Slowly bend your elbows and lower the barbell in a semicircle from the starting point until it touches the back of your neck. Return the barbell along the same arc to the starting position, and repeat for the required number of repetitions.

4. Training Tip—This exercise is often done with a single dumbbell held in both hands.

Standing Triceps Extension—finish and start.

Reverse Curl

1. **Emphasis**—This movement puts a strong stress on both the brachialis muscle under your biceps and the muscles of your forearms.

2. **Starting Position**—Grasp a barbell with a shoulder-width grip, and stand erect so the barbell rests across the tops of your thighs. Your palms should be facing your body. Press your upper arms against the sides of your torso, and keep them in that position throughout the movement.

3. **The Movement**—Slowly curl the barbell in a semicircle from your thighs to your chin. Lower along the same arc back to the starting point, and repeat for the required number of repetitions.

4. **Training Tip**—For variety, you can use a narrow grip in the middle of the barbell instead of the shoulder-width grip.

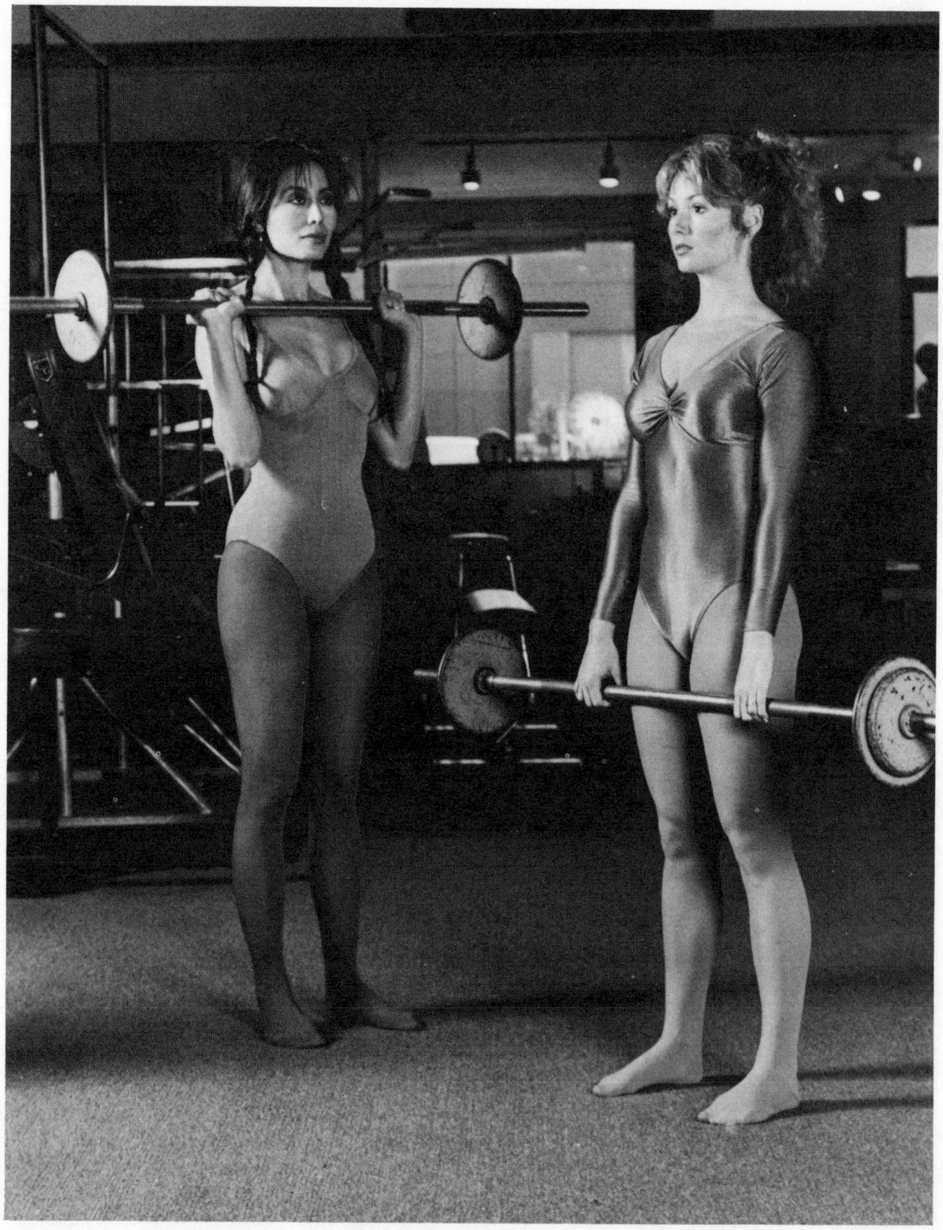

Reverse Curl—finish and start.

Dumbbell Wrist Curl

1. Emphasis—This movement stresses all of the muscles of your forearms.

2. Starting Position—Grasp a single dumbbell and run the forearm of your exercising hand along the top of a flat exercise bench so your wrist and hand hang off the edge of the bench. You can either sit on the bench or kneel beside it. Sag your wrist—either palm up or palm down—downward as far as possible.

3. The Movement—Curl the dumbbell upward in a small semicircle as high as you can. Lower back to the starting point, and repeat for the required number of repetitions.

4. Training Tip—This movement can also be done with two dumbbells at once, running your forearms down your thighs as you did for a standard Barbell Wrist Curl movement.

Dumbbell Wrist Curl—start (left) and finish (right).

Dumbbell Wrist Curl using two dumbbells—midpoint.

INTERMEDIATE/ADVANCED ROUTINES

The training programs in this section will be divided into two parts—intermediate and advanced routines. All of the intermediate routines (Table 5-1) are designed to be used three days per week, while the advanced programs (Table 5-2) are intended to be used with a four-day split routine. All routines are made up with the three major types of resistance training equipment—free weights, Nautilus machines, and Universal Gym machines. If you can't do an exercise that's listed with the equipment you have, simply substitute in an equivalent movement.

TABLE 5-1 Intermediate Routines

Body Shaping

Exercise	Sets	Reps
1. Leg Raise	2-3	25-50
2. Seated Twisting	2-3	50-100
3. Toe Raise on Nautilus Omni	5	15-20
4. Squat	4	10-15
5. Let Curl	3	10-15
6. Nautilus Hip & Back	2	10-15
7. Seated Pulley Row	3	8-12
8. Nautilus Behind Neck	2	8-12
9. Upright Row	3	8-12
10. Bench Press	3	6-10
11. Incline Flyes	2	8-12
12. Press Behind Neck	3	6-10
13. Side Laterals	2	8-12
14. Incline Curl	3	8-12
15. Nautilus Multi Position Triceps	3	8-12
16. Dumbbell Wrist Curl	4	15-20

Weight Gaining

Exercise	Sets	Reps
1. Leg Raise	3	25-50
2. Seated Calf Machine	5	15/12/10/8/6*
3. Squat	6	12/10/8/6/4/2*
4. Deadlifts	3	10/8/6*
5. Seated Pulley Row	5	12/10/8/6/4*
6. Shrug	3	12/10/8*
7. Incline Press	5	12/10/8/6/4*
8. Flyes	3	12/10/8*
9. Press Behind Neck	4	10/8/6/4*
10. Nautilus Multi Position Curl	3	10/8/6*
11. Standing Triceps Extension	3	10/8/6*
12. Barbell Wrist Curl	4	15-20

* Pyramid these.

Strength Improvement

Exercise	Sets	Reps
1. Situps (with weight behind head)	3	15/12/10*
2. Squats	6	8/6/6/4/4/2*
3. Deadlifts	4	6/5/4/3*
4. Barbell Bent Rowing	5	10/8/6/5/4*
5. Shrug	4	10/8/6/4*
6. Bench Press	6	8/6/5/4/3/2*
7. Military Press	4	6/5/4/3*
8. Barbell Curl	3	8/6/5*
9. Lying Triceps Extension	3	8/6/5*
10. Seated Calf Machine	3	12/10/8*
11. Standing Calf Machine	3	12/10/8*
12. Dumbbell Wrist Curl	4	12/10/8/6*

* Pyramid these.

Sports Performance Improvement

Exercise	Sets	Reps
1. Situps	2	25-50
2. Leg Raise	2	25-50
3. Seated Twisting	2	50-100
4. Seated Calf Machine	3	15-20
5. Standing Calf Machine	3	15-20
6. Squat	2	10-15
7. Leg Extension	2	10-15
8. Leg Curl	2	10-15
9. Nautilus Hip & Back	2	8-12
10. Nautilus Pullover	2	8-12
11. Dumbbell Bent Row	2	8-12
12. Upright Row	2	8-12
13. Incline Dumbbell Press	3	6-10
14. Decline Flyes	2	8-12
15. Dumbbell Press	2	6-10
16. Side Laterals	2	8-12
17. Concentration Curl	3	8-12
18. Pulley Pushdown	3	8-12
19. Reverse Curl	2	8-12
20. Dumbbell Wrist Curl	3	15-20

Table 5-2 begins on next page.

TABLE 5-2 Advanced Routines

Body Toning

Monday-Thursday

Exercise	Sets	Reps
1. Leg Raise	3	25-50
2. Seated Twisting	2	50-100
3. Standing Calf Machine	4	15-20
4. Leg Press	3	10-15
5. Leg Extension	2	10-15
6. Leg Curl	2	10-15
7. Hyperextension	3	10-15
8. Dumbbell Shrugs	3	10-15
9. Nautilus Row	3	10-15
10. Lat Pulldown	2	8-12
11. Barbell Curl	3	8-12
12. Reverse Curl	2	8-12
13. Barbell Wrist Curl	4	15-20

Tuesday-Friday

Exercise	Sets	Reps
1. Situps	3	25-50
2. Seated Twisting	2	50-100
3. Seated Calf Machine	4	15-20
4. Incline Press	3	6-10
5. Flyes (flat bench)	2	8-12
6. Decline Flyes	2	8-12
7. Nautilus Seated Press	3	6-10
8. Side Laterals	2	8-12
9. Lying Triceps Extension	2	8-12
10. Nautilus Multi Triceps	2	8-12
11. Dumbbell Wrist Curl	4	15-20

Weight Gaining

Monday-Thursday

Exercise	Sets	Reps
1. Situps	2	25-50
2. Seated Twisting	1	50-100
3. Hyperextension	2	10-15
4. Squat	5	12/10/8/6/4*
5. Leg Curl	3	8-12
6. Nautilus Pullover	4	12/10/8/6*
7. Dumbbell Bent Row	3	10/8/6*
8. Incline Curl	3	10/8/6*
9. Reverse Curl	3	10/8/6*
10. Barbell Wrist Curl	4	15/12/10/8*
11. Nautilus Omni Calf Raise	4	15/12/10/8*

Tuesday-Friday

Exercise	Sets	Reps
1. Leg Raise	3	25-50
2. Bench Press	4	10/8/6/4*
3. Incline Flyes	3	10/8/6*
4. Universal Seated Press	4	8/6/4/2*
5. Upright Row	3	10/8/6*
6. Lying Triceps Extension	4	10/8/6/4*
7. Dumbbell Wrist Curl	4	15/12/10/8*
8. Seated Calf Machine	4	15/12/10/8*

* Pyramid these.

Strength Improvement

Monday-Thursday

Exercise	Sets	Reps
1. Leg Raise (off bench)	3	20-25
2. Deadlift	4	8/6/4/2*
3. Squat	6	8/6/5/4/3/2*
4. Shrug	4	10/8/6/4*
5. Nautilus Pullover	5	10/8/6/5/4*
6. Nautilus Multi Curl	4	8/6/5/4*
7. Barbell Wrist Curl	4	10/8/6/6*
8. Standing Calf Machine	5	12/10/8/6/4*

Tuesday-Friday

Exercise	Sets	Reps
1. Weighted Situps	3	12/10/8*
2. Incline Press	5	10/8/6/4/2*
3. Bench Press	3	8/6/4*
4. Press Behind Neck	4	8/6/4/2*
5. Upright Row	3	8/6/4*
6. Lying Triceps Extension	3	8/6/4*
7. Barbell Reverse Wrist Curl	4	10/8/6/6*
8. Seated Calf Machine	5	12/10/8/6/4*

* Pyramid these.

Sports Performance Improvement

Monday-Thursday

Exercise	Sets	Reps
1. Situps	3	25-50
2. Seated Twisting	2	50-100
3. Standing Calf Machine	3	15-20
4. Calf Press	2	15-20
5. Hyperextension	2-3	10-15
6. Seated Pulley Row	3	8-12
7. Nautilus Behind Neck	2	8-12

8. Upright Row	3	8-12
9. Incline Dumbbell Press	3	6-10
10. Flyes (flat bench)	2	8-12
11. Decline Flyes	2	8-12
12. Dumbbell Press	3	6-10
13. Side Laterals	2	8-12
14. Reverse Curl	2	8-12
15. Dumbbell Wrist Curl	2	10-15

Tuesday-Friday

Exercises	Sets	Reps
1. Leg Raise	3	25-50
2. Seated Twisting	2	50-100
3. Leg Press	3	10-15
4. Leg Extension	2	10-15
5. Leg Curl	2	10-15
6. Pulley Curl	2	8-12
7. Concentration Curl	2	8-12
8. Standing Triceps Extension	2	8-12
9. Pulley Pushdown	2	8-12
10. Barbell Reverse Wrist Curl	4	10-15

By the time you have finished using all of the training schedules in this chapter you will know enough about your body to easily be able to make up your own individualized routines.

ONWARD

In Chapter 6 we will discuss the art and sport of competitive bodybuilding for women. While this branch of weight training is not for everyone, some women will find bodybuilding to be highly challenging and rewarding.

Stacey Bentley uses Flyes to prime her "pump."

Rachel McLish, 1980 Ms. Olympia, uses Dumbbell Bent Rows to thicken her back, shoulder, and arm muscles.

6
Competitive Bodybuilding

Competitive bodybuilding isn't for every woman! But for the rare women who choses to train and diet for bodybuilding competition, a whole new world opens up. She becomes an elite person who can endure long hours of super-intense workouts, weeks of strict dieting, and a lifetime of disciplined living.

To reach the top in competitive bodybuilding you must dedicate yourself 100 percent to the quest. You must be able to totally discipline yourself to avoid junk foods, reduce the amount of time you spend with your friends, and even place your boyfriend, husband, and family second in your life to bodybuilding. And if you are not able to make such sacrifices, you should forget about competing and settle for training just to stay in shape.

If you can discipline yourself, however, and if you are willing to put in five or more years of build-up training, you will open up a tremendously rewarding career. Many champion bodybuilders are making a living through bodybuilding. If you can do it, go for the gold yourself!

CYCLE TRAINING

Competitive bodybuilders cycle their training by alternating two- to nine-month periods of heavy workouts to build muscle mass with six- to twelve-week periods of lighter training to bring out muscular detail. And hand-in-hand with cycling their training they also cycle their diets (see the next section), which helps them to achieve maximum muscularity and muscle mass onstage at a competition.

In order to build muscle mass in the off-season, you should train as heavy as possible four days per week, using primarily basic exercises and doing four to six sets of five to eight reps per movement. There is a direct relationship between the amount of weight you use in each exercise and the size of your muscles, so you must essentially power train to build appreciable muscle mass. Most outstanding competitive bodybuilders will be strong enough to Bench Press their body weight four to six times and Squat with one-and-a-half to two times their body weight for four to six repetitions.

Utilizing the above guidelines, Table 6-1 presents a typical off-season bodybuilding training program.

TABLE 6-1 Typical Off-Season Bodybuilding Program

Monday-Thursday

Exercise	Sets	Reps
1. Situps	3	25-50
2. Leg Raise	3	25-50
3. Seated Twisting	3	50-100
4. Bench Press	5	8/7/6/5/4*
5. Incline Dumbbell Press	4	8/7/6/5*
6. Press Behind Neck	4	8/7/6/5*
7. Upright Row	4	8/7/6/5*
8. Nautilus Pullover	5	8/7/6/5/4*
9. Lat Pulldown	4	8/7/6/5*
10. Standing Calf Machine	5-8	10-15
11. Barbell Wrist Curl	3	15-20
12. Barbell Reverse Wrist Curl	3	15-20

Tuesday-Friday

Exercise	Sets	Reps
1. Situps	3	25-50
2. Leg Raise	3	25-50
3. Seated Twisting	3	50-100
4. Squat	5	10/8/6/5/4*
5. Leg Extension	3	10-12
6. Leg Curl	3	10-12
7. Barbell Curl	3	8/6/5*
8. Nautilus Curl	3	8/6/5*
9. Lying Triceps Extension	3	8/6/5*
10. Nautilus Triceps Extension	3	8/6/5*
11. Seated Calf Machine	5-8	10-15
12. Dumbbell Wrist Curl	3	15-20
13. Dumbbell Reverse Wrist Curl	3	15-20

* Pyramid these.

About eight weeks before competing, you should begin to work gradually into a precompetition cycle by starting to train six days per week, working each muscle group twice a week, (calves, abs, and forearms can be trained four to six times per week). You should also begin to include isolation exercises in your routines, do higher repetitions (eight to twelve reps), do a few more total sets per muscle group (eight to twelve sets) and train slightly faster (45 to 60 seconds rest between sets, versus 60 to 75 seconds in the off-season).

Using the above guidelines, Table 6-2 is a typical first-level precompetitive exercise program.

TABLE 6-2 Precompetitive Program

Monday-Thursday

Exercise	Sets	Reps
1. Situps	4	25-50
2. Leg Raises	4	25-50
3. Seated Twisting	4	50-100
4. Seated Calf Machine	4-5	10-15
5. Calf Raise on Nautilus Omni	4-5	10-15
6. Incline Press	4	8-10
7. Flat Flyes	3	10-12
8. Decline Flyes	3	10-12
9. Dumbbell Press	3	8-10
10. Side Lateral Raise	3	10-12
11. Upright Row	3	10-12
12. Standing Triceps Extension	3	10-12
13. Pulley Pushdown	3	10-12
14. Barbell Wrist Curl	3	15-20
15. Barbell Reverse Wrist Curl	3	15-20

Tuesday-Friday

Exercise	Sets	Reps
1. Situps	4	25-50
2. Leg Raises	4	25-50
3. Seated Twisting	4	50-100
4. Dumbbell Bent Row	4	8-10
5. Nautilus Pullover	3	10-12
6. Lat Pulldown	3	10-12
7. Shrug	3	10-15
8. Hyperextension	3	10-15
9. Cable Curl	3	10-12
10. Concentration Curl	3	10-12
11. Dumbbell Wrist Curl	3	15-20
12. Dumbbell Reverse Wrist Curl	3	15-20
13. Standing Calf Machine	4-5	10-15
14. Calf Press	4-5	10-15

Wednesday-Saturday

Exercise	Sets	Reps
1. Situps	4	25-50
2. Leg Raises	4	25-50
3. Seated Twisting	4	50-100
4. Squat	4	10-15
5. Leg Press	3	10-15
6. Leg Extension	3	10-15
7. Leg Curl	4	10-15
8. Standing Calf Machine	4-5	10-15
9. Seated Calf Machine	4-5	10-15
10. Reverse Curl	3	10-12

After four weeks on the above routines—or about four weeks before competing—you should make another intensity jump by beginning to train each major muscle group three times per week on a six-day split. You can also begin using the intensity techniques discussed in Chapter 4—supersets, forced reps, etc.—to further intensify your workouts.

You should be resting only 30 to 40 seconds between sets to utilize fully the Weider *Quality Training* principle. This faster training—coupled with the strict diet you will be on—will force you to use lighter poundages for each exercise. This is normal, but you should still try to use the heaviest possible workout poundages, even if they are much lighter than what you use in the off-season.

Using brackets to designate exercises that you can superset, Table 6-3 gives you a sample second-level precontest workout program.

TABLE 6-3 Second-Level Precontest Program

Monday-Wednesday-Friday

Exercise	Sets	Reps
1. Situps	5	25–50
2. Leg Raises	5	25–50
3. Seated Twisting	5	50–100
4. Standing Calf Machine	4–5	10–15
5. Calf Press	4–5	15–20
6. Incline Dumbbell Press	4	10–12
7. Flat Flyes	4	10–12
8. Decline Flyes	4	10–12
9. Press Behind Neck	4	8–10
10. Side Laterals	3	10–12
11. Seated Press	3	8–10
12. Nautilus Triceps Extension	4	10–12
13. Pulley Pushdown	3	10–12
14. Barbell Wrist Curl	4	15–20
15. Barbell Reverse Wrist Curl	4	15–20

Tuesday-Thursday-Saturday

Exercise	Sets	Reps
1. Situps	5	25–50
2. Leg Raises	5	25–50
3. Seated Twisting	5	50–100
4. Squat	4	10–15
5. Leg Press	3	10–15
6. Leg Extension	4	10–15
7. Leg Curl	4	10–15
8. Dumbbell Bent Row	4	10–12
9. Lat Pulldown	3	10–12
10. Nautilus Pullover	3	10–12
11. Shrug	3	10–15
12. Hyperextension	3	10–15
13. Incline Curl	3	10–15
14. Concentration Curl	3	10–12
15. Dumbbell Wrist Curl	4	10–15
16. Dumbbell Reverse Wrist Curl	4	10–15
17. Seated Calf Machine	4–5	10–15
18. Calf Raise on Nautilus Omni	4–5	15–20

Notice that at each of the three discussed intensity levels we've asked you to do more abdominal work. This increased abdominal training is a key factor in precontest training, because—combined with a precontest diet and aerobic workouts—it will result in the smallest possible waist measurement. If your waist is not as small as it should be, you might even consider hitting your abs twice per day, doing three to five sets of each movement in the morning and three to five more sets of each exercise at night.

For the last three to six weeks before a contest, you might wish to do a 30- to 45-minute aerobic workout each day in addition to your bodybuilding session. This aerobic training can consist of running, bicycling, dancing, or an aerobic calisthenics exercise session to music. Regardless of the activity, such aerobic workouts will burn up extra calories and result in a greater precontest body fat loss.

If you want to reach the ultimate in precontest training intensity—and we recommend this technique only to national- and international-level competitors—you can use the Weider *Double-Split Routine* training principle. This consists of doing two bodybuilding workouts per day, one in the morning and one in the late afternoon or evening, plus your normal aerobic session sometime during the day.

Since you will have limited energy during your precontest cycle, it is often difficult to do a full workout for every body part. But if you do two shorter workouts each day, you'll have plenty of energy for the morning session, plus sufficient recovery time to bounce back for the second workout later in the day.

Using a double split also seems to result in a faster body weight loss than if the same amount of work is done in a single session. This is caused by two factors: you can train harder and more intensely in a shorter workout; and training more frequently stimulates the body's Basal Metabolic Rate (BMR), which forces your body to burn more fat for daily body maintenance energy requirements.

Here is a schematic of a Weider *Double-Split Routine,* into which you can plug the foregoing individual body-part workouts for the final week or two of precontest training:

Monday-Wednesday-Friday (AM)	Monday-Wednesday-Friday (PM)
Abdominals	Abdominals
Calves	Forearms
Chest	Deltoids
Triceps	Biceps

Tuesday-Thursday-Saturday (AM)	Tuesday-Thursday-Saturday (PM)
Abdominals	Abdominals
Forearms	Calves
Thighs	Back

By cycling your workouts from off-season training through two or three precontest intensity levels—and by including a strict precontest diet and daily aerobic sessions—you can build appreciable muscle mass and then strip off the body's superfluous fat to reveal a maximum degree of muscular detail. And when you can do this perfectly, you should be a contest winner.

CYCLE DIETING

While you are cycling your training programs during the year, you should also cycle your diet. In the off-season you can eat fairly loosely, which will result in body weight gain consisting of both muscle and fat, but prior to a contest you must diet very strictly to reduce your body-fat levels to a minimum.

In the off-season, you should eat a balanced diet but avoid junk foods. While individual caloric requirements vary, you can probably safely consume 2,500 calories per day, which will give you plenty of energy for your heavy, muscle-building off-season workouts.

You can eat such high-fat foods as beef, pork, eggs, and milk products in the off-season. You should also consume plenty of natural complex carbohydrate foods, such as fresh fruits, whole grains, salads, and fresh vegetables. These foods will give you a high energy level, plus yield plenty of natural vitamins and minerals.

A precontest diet should be initiated six to twelve weeks before a competition. The exact point at which you start dieting will depend on how much fat you are carrying on your body. Naturally, you will need to diet for a longer period of time if you have a lot of fat and less time if you are fairly lean to begin with. Allow about one week of dieting for each one-and-a-half to two pounds of fat you will need to lose.

Once you begin a precontest diet, it should be made progressively stricter as time goes on. If you jumped right into a very strict diet, it would be too much of a shock to your body. You would probably become physically ill, or you would develop food cravings and soon fall off the diet. But by easing into a tight diet, you won't develop such problems.

As you diet, keep an eye on how you look in the mirror, noting your appearance at specific checkpoints prior to competing, as well as how various caloric intake levels and food combinations effect the appearance of your body. With several competition cycles, these observations will allow you to develop an instinct for precontest dieting. Then you can adjust your diet according to how you look at each checkpoint, which allows you to peak perfectly for each contest you enter.

When you begin your diet, first cut out all junk foods that might have sneaked into your daily meals. Next, reduce and then eliminate grains, followed by milk products, eggs, beef, pork, and high-fat vegetables and fruits like corn and avocados.

At its tightest, your diet should consist of broiled fish, baked or broiled chicken breasts (without the skin, which is very high in fat), turkey white meat, salads, fresh fruits, and fresh vegetables. You should drink only water and unsweetened iced or hot tea, since diet sodas are high in sodium content, and sodium retains excess water in the body. Even coffee is a no-no, because caffeine releases insulin in the body, causing false hunger pangs.

As we have already mentioned, the severity of your diet will depend on how much body fat you are carrying as your competition approaches. While some women bodybuilders go as low as 400 to 500 calories per day, you will probably find that 1000 to 1200 calories a day will strip all of the fat from your body in only three to five weeks. Even that "high" of a caloric intake will be difficult to maintain, however, since it can result in low energy levels, particularly in combination with three to five hours of training each day.

When you are on a very strict diet, it is difficult to take in sufficient vitamins for optimum health, particularly when you are also making severe physical demands on your body. Therefore, you should increase your intake of vitamins and minerals through food supplements as your diet tightens up. Just prior to competing, you will probably need two to three times the amount of each vitamin and mineral as you needed in the off-season.

While we heartily recommend the use of protein supplements (tablets, powders, and liquid amino acids) during the off-season building cycle, you should stop using them two or three weeks before competing. These supplements tend to retain water in the body, which can be a disaster when you're trying to achieve maximum muscularity for a show. Excess water in your body will actually make you look *fat*, so take every possible measure to prevent water retention before a competition.

HOW TO WATCH/ENTER A COMPETITION

Under the aegis of the American Federation of Women Bodybuilders (AFWB), literally scores of amateur bodybuilding competitions are held around the country each year. And there are also several high-level professional bodybuilding shows staged for women each year.

Eventually, you will want to enter a local or state competition, working your way up through the ranks to regional and finally national and international competition. If you are good enough and luck is on your side, you may eventually win the Ms. America title (amateur bodybuilding's most prestigious award) or even one of the hotly contested pro titles.

If you want to compete, we recommend that you first attend several women's bodybuilding shows as a spectator. This will allow you to familiarize yourself with how these shows are run and judged, as well as with how the various contestants pose, before you actually compete. Such knowledge acquired beforehand will save you plenty of embarrassment and grief during your first competitive effort.

Almost all women's bodybuilding contests (which are advertised each month in *Muscle & Fitness* magazine) are prejudged, since the judging procedure can take several hours to complete. Although a few prejudgings are closed to the public, most contest promoters try to make a little extra money by opening them to the public and charging a small admission fee. If the prejudging is open to the public, be sure to attend it, since this is where all of the real action takes place at a bodybuilding competition.

There will be either five or seven judges—usually seven—at each prejudging. These are invariably men and women with vast backgrounds in the sport, and most of the best national and international judges began judging at the local level and rose through the ranks themselves as a result of their abilities and impartiality. While an occasional incompetent judge will be included on a judging panel (usually at the local or state level), you will almost always be judged fairly, particularly at the regional, national, and international competitive levels.

Each judge scores every contestant. And to prevent favoritism or downright incompetence from unfairly helping or hurting a contestant, the high and low scores given to each contestant are thrown out, and the remaining three or five scores are added up for the final score and placing.

The contestants are judged both in groups and as individuals in three rounds of posing and strictly on an individual basis in one more, and scores are given for each judging round. The final combined score for each contestant is determined by adding up her scores for each of the four judging rounds.

In Round One, the contestants stand individually in relaxed attitudes from the front, right side, back, and left side. Then they are brought out as a group and compared to each other before scores are assessed. This round gives the judges a general idea of how each woman looks. They can assess her muscle mass, body symmetry (general shape, plus balance from side to side), proportions (size relationships of all body parts), muscle tone (tightness and absence of body fat), grooming (tan, hair, skin quality, etc.), and general appearance.

Round Two consists of six standardized compulsory poses—front and back poses with the arms held above shoulder height, front and back poses with the arms held below the shoulders, and a pose from each side. Again, the contestants are viewed individually and then compared in groups. Round Two allows the judges to refine their initial impressions from Round One, as well as to see how each individual muscle group looks under tension. Because the six compulsory poses are standardized, general

Rachel McLish (center) won the 1980 U.S. Women's Bodybuilding Championships. Claudia Wilbourn (right) was second, and Georgia Miller Fudge (left) took third.

posing ability is less of a factor in Round Two than is pure muscular development.

In Round Three posing ability comes to the fore as each contestant is allowed one minute for individual free posing. Here each woman can insert her personality, athletic ability, dance skills, and creative talents into a posing routine. The variety of posing styles—as well as the general level of posing ability—at women's competitions is astounding. We dare to say that female bodybuilders have advanced the art of physique presentation much further than their male counterparts!

Round Four consists of a pose-down between the top five contestants. For one or two minutes they pose as a group, virtually slugging it out among themselves for first-place honors. This round is usually conducted at the evening public show, since it is invariably the most exciting and competitive round of judging.

Prior to Round Four, each contestant has had her scores from the first three judging rounds totaled, with 300 points being a perfect score. This is how the five finalists are picked. Then in Round Four each judge picks his or her choice for first place, and one point is added to each contestant's base score for every first-place vote. And when the scores are either tied or very

The 1980 Ms. Olympia contest.

1980 Ms. Olympia finalists: (left to right) Corrine Machado-Ching (4th), Auby Paulik (2nd), Lynn Conkwright (3rd), Rachel McLish (1st), and Stacey Bentley (5th).

close after three rounds, the pose-down can be decisive.

Finally, trophies are awarded to the first three or five contestants, as well as occasionally for such special categories as Best Poser, Most Symmetrical, and Best Muscle Tone. And when you finally stand on the winners' platform to receive your initial first-place award, you will know what competitive bodybuilding is all about. It is the ecstasy of victory following the agony of several defeats on the way up!

POSING

All four rounds of posing must be regularly practiced, even the "relaxed" stances in Round One, although the majority of your time should be spent perfecting your free-posing. This is because free-posing is the height of the bodybuilding art form, and your posing for each of the other three rounds can be improved merely by practicing your Round Three routine.

By studying the photos of champion women bodybuilders in *Muscle & Fitness* and *Shape* plus observing how women pose at a bodybuilding show or two, you can begin to develop poses that suit your individual body. Just pick a pose and imitate it in the mirror, trying slightly different body positions than what you see in the picture to adapt the pose to your individual body. With a few weeks of practice, you will be able to master 15 to 20 poses, which is enough for a basic free-posing routine.

Once you have chosen 15 to 20 poses, you will need to arrange them so you can flow with esthetic transitions from pose to pose. Observe the transitions of better contestants at a bodybuilding show, and gradually work their moves into your own routine. This should be fairly easy for you, particularly if you have a dance and/or gymnastics background.

You won't be able to develop a good free-posing routine overnight. It should take several weeks—even months—but once you have worked up an effective and charismatic free-posing routine, you'll be several giant steps closer to winning your first title.

The poses in Round One really *are* poses, since they are held under a degree of muscle tension, even if they are supposed to be done relaxed. With practice, you will also find tiny shifts of leg, arm, and torso position that will enhance each of the four stances. Sometimes even a five-degree twist at the waist will improve one of the poses 50 percent. So spend a few minutes each day practicing your Round One poses.

You should also practice the six compulsory poses from Round Two on a daily basis. These poses will probably form the foundation of your free-posing routine, but you should practice each one nonetheless. And you should develop and practice transitions between each of the compulsory poses.

The posedown round is difficult to practice, short of actually being involved in two or three of them. You will need a more quickly moving routine for Round Four, however, because the quicker movements tend to catch a judge's eye more often than slower movements. And the most aggressive-appearing woman often garners a majority of first-place votes in Round Four, so you should regularly practice posing more forcefully and quickly for Round Four.

In its essence, posing is an extension of your personality. You will live and die with your posing, and no amount of training and dieting can compensate for a timid and ineffective posing routine. So, you would do well to devote at least 30 to 60 minutes per day to practicing your posing when you have a show coming up.

CONTEST GROOMING AND TANNING

Your general appearance is important at a contest, so you should note how women contestants groom themselves for competition. Note the most effective uses of makeup, hair style, and choice of posing attire, and then base your own grooming efforts on these observations.

Generally speaking, you will need to use heavier-than-normal makeup—the same as stage actresses must use—because you will be 15 or more feet from the judging panel and even further from the audience. At such distances light makeup won't be visible.

You can wear a flower in your hair to highlight your hairstyle, but avoid all jewelry at a competition, except perhaps your wedding ring. If you wear jewelry, you will only distract the judges and audience from looking at and evaluating your muscular development. In the same vein, choose a posing suit of a solid color that harmonizes with your own coloring. Wearing patt-

On the following pages, we present Rachel McLish posing. Note her skin tone as well as her choice of attire and hairstyle.

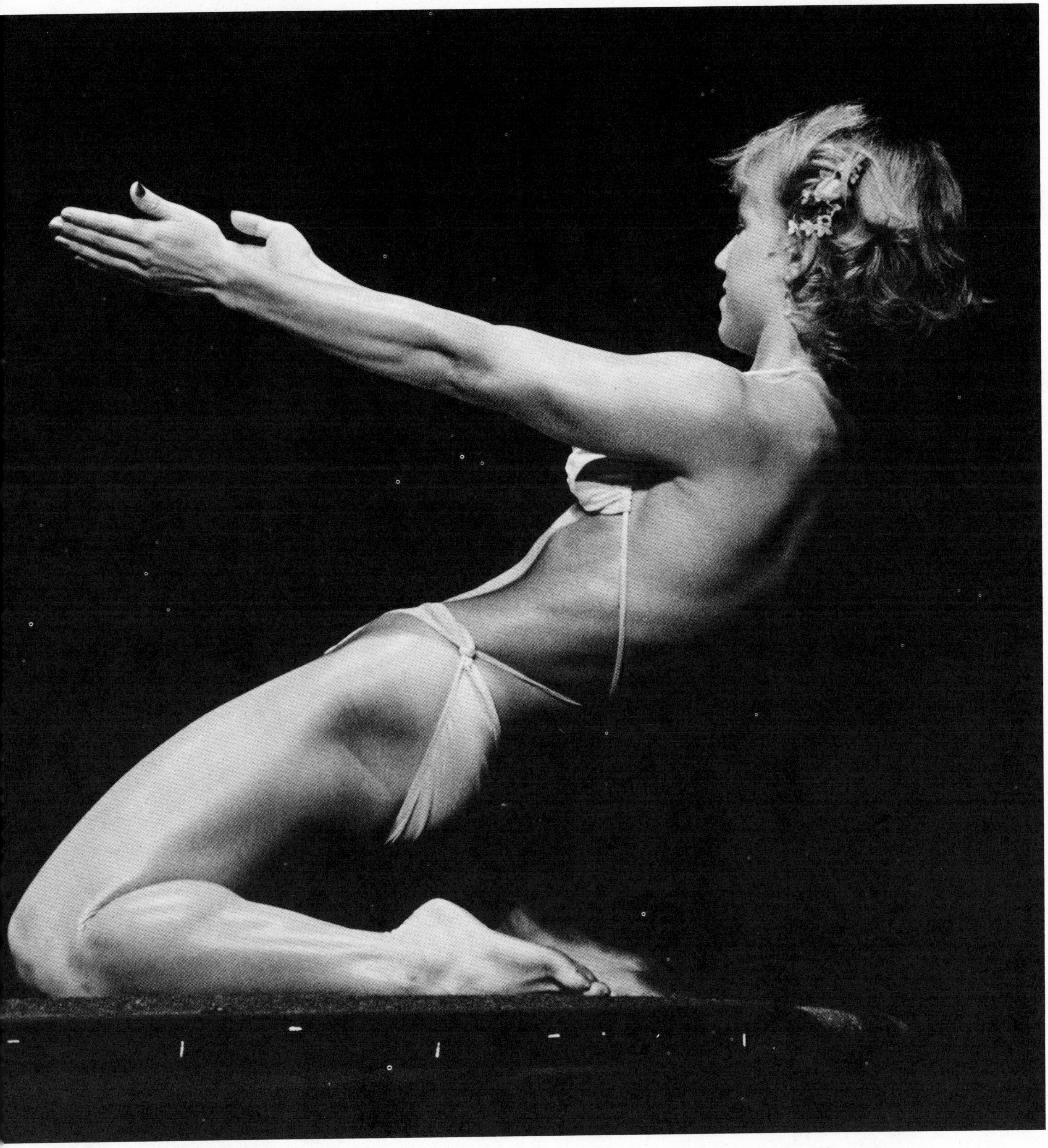

Stacey Bentley posing.

erned or garishly colored posing suits will also detract from your physique.

Unless you are a black woman, an even, deep, and natural tan can be the most important factor in your grooming program. A good tan makes you look much healthier and more vibrant than if you went into a show with pale skin. A dark tan can also camoflage a blotchy skin, and it makes anyone's body—man or woman—look much harder than normal.

Begin lying out in the sun with a 20-minute session six to eight weeks before competing. Be sure to use a good tanning oil, so your skin doesn't dry out. Gradually increase the length of your exposure to the sun, and *never* miss a day in the sun. By sunning daily for six to eight weeks, you'll be able to acquire a deep, even tan all over your body.

If you live where the sun isn't out much or if it's winter, you can try using a booth at one of the many tanning salons springing up all over the country. Artificial light won't give you as good of a tan as natural sunlight, but such a salon tan will be superior to anything you can get with quick-tan chemical preparations.

As a last resort, you can use chemical tanning agents to get some degree of skin coloring during the winter. Two or three coats of tanning cream will give you a fairly decent—albeit yellowish—skin coloring. Just be sure to wear rubber gloves when applying the cream, since it will stain your hands an ugly orange color. You should also be careful not to get the cream on your posing suit, because it will also stain cloth!

BODYBUILDING DRUGS

Unfortunately, a few exceedingly foolish women bodybuilders have begun to use dangerous anabolic steroids (artificial male hormones) to increase their degree of muscle mass for competitions. This is even dangerous to male bodybuilders, and for a female bodybuilder to use steroids opens her up to calamitous side effects.

The ultimate side effect of steroid usage is death. Numerous scientific studies have linked steroid usage to cancer incidence and particularly to cancer of the liver, kidneys, and bladder. Other severe side effects that a woman can experience include masculinization (particularly of a fetus if you are pregnant and taking steroids), hair loss, hair growth all over the body, beard growth, water retention, menstrual irregularities, clitoral enlargement, and wild mood swings.

It is our opinion that anabolic steroids have no place in women's bodybuilding, nor in men's bodybuilding either for that matter. The small amount of muscle tissue that they might give you is definitely not worth the risk to your health that steroids present. In the long run, you can build maximum muscle mass and detail with hard training and a sensible approach to bodybuilding nutrition. And if you add muscle to your body this way, you do so while improving—not harming—your health.

MENTAL APPROACH

At the top levels of bodybuilding—or any other sport—the mind plays a tremendous role in reaching one's ultimate physical potential. In fact, you can actually program your mind to assist you in developing a championship physique.

Overall, your mental approach to bodybuilding should be *positive*. Always convince yourself that you will reach your goals in the sport if you discipline yourself to train hard and regularly, rest optimally, and constantly monitor your diet. Never allow yourself to think for a minute that you will ever fail.

To program your mind for success, you can use a technique called *visualization*. This amounts to systematically daydreaming about how you one day want to look. This takes advantage of a psychological technique called self-actualization. You simply convince your subconscious mind that you will one day look the way you imagine yourself, and then your subconscious automatically makes choices for you. Thus, a half pound of broiled fish actually begins to taste better to you than an ice cream cone, and your workouts become pure pleasure instead of drudgery.

To get the most out of the visualization process, you must do it daily, preferably just before you fall asleep each night. Visualizing at bedtime promotes regularity, and the visualization process results in a subconscious "fix" more easily when you're fully relaxed and free from the day's frequent distractions.

As you are lying in bed, build a mental picture of your body the way you know it will one day be. Imagine every tiny muscle, every peak, and every valley, almost as if you were seeing an image of your body projected onto a movie screen.

At first it will be difficult to focus on this image for more than a minute at a time, because your mind will tend to wander. If you jerk your-

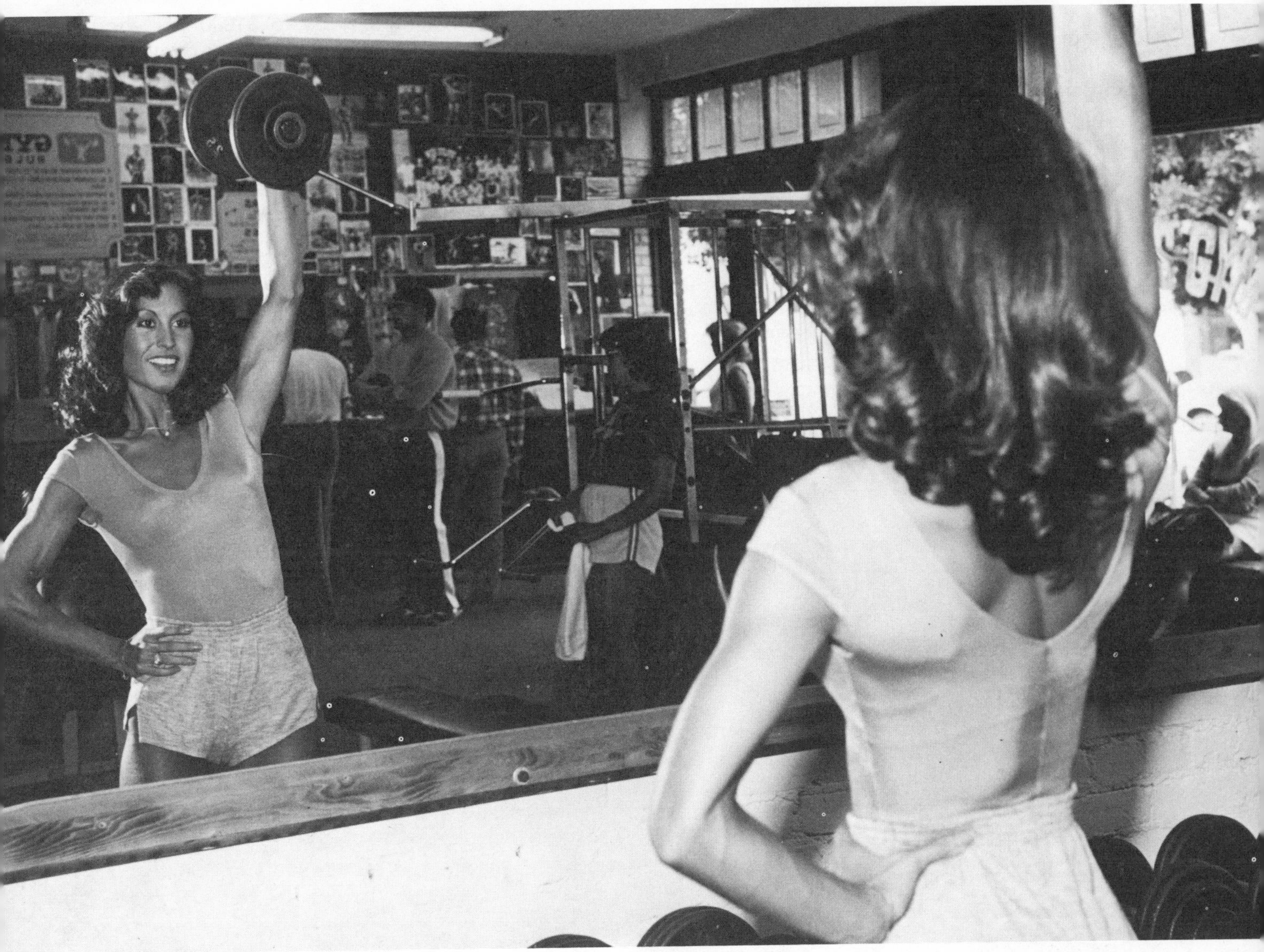

Rachel McLish demonstrates another mental approach to weight lifting. By exercising in front of a mirror, she can monitor her exercise form and visualize the blood pumping into her muscles.

self back to your image every time your attention wanders, however, you will quickly build the ability to concentrate exclusively on your image for a full 15 minutes, the length of time required to fully condition your subconscious mind.

While visualization is a technique used primarily by competing bodybuilders, even beginners and intermediates can use it to reach their goals. And you can also use this mind-programming technique to help yourself reach goals in any aspect of your life. All you need to do is daydream consistently and creatively, and you can reach any realistic goal!

PROFESSIONAL BODYBUILDING

Several outstanding women bodybuilders are actually making a living from the sport, and many more will be able to do so in the future. A couple of the top women bodybuilders are even making a small fortune from bodybuilding.

For the best bodybuilders, there are a number of sources of income related to our sport. The most obvious of these is prize money won in pro competitions. First prize in the bigger pro shows is between $5000 and $10,000, and even fifth place can bring a woman $1000 to $2500 in prize money. In future years there will be more and more pro shows for women, and the prize money at each show will increase dramatically within the next five years.

If a woman has won a major title, she will be in demand as a guest poser at lower-level amateur shows. For each exhibition she can command a fee of $500 to $1000 (plus expenses), and a top woman bodybuilder can easily schedule 10 or more such exhibitions per year. Even minor champions can pick up three to five exhibitions each year.

Training seminars ($250 to $1000 per shot) are a third source of income. Many gyms with large female memberships have scheduled Rachel McLish, Laura Combes, Stacy Bentley, and other champion bodybuilders for training seminars. In future years—as competitive bodybuilding continues to explode in popularity—these seminars will become increasingly lucrative.

By swimming in the ocean, Rachel gets in her aerobic workouts as well as that all-important exposure to the sun.

Rachel uses a dumbbell for Close-Grip Upright Rows, an excellent shoulder developer.

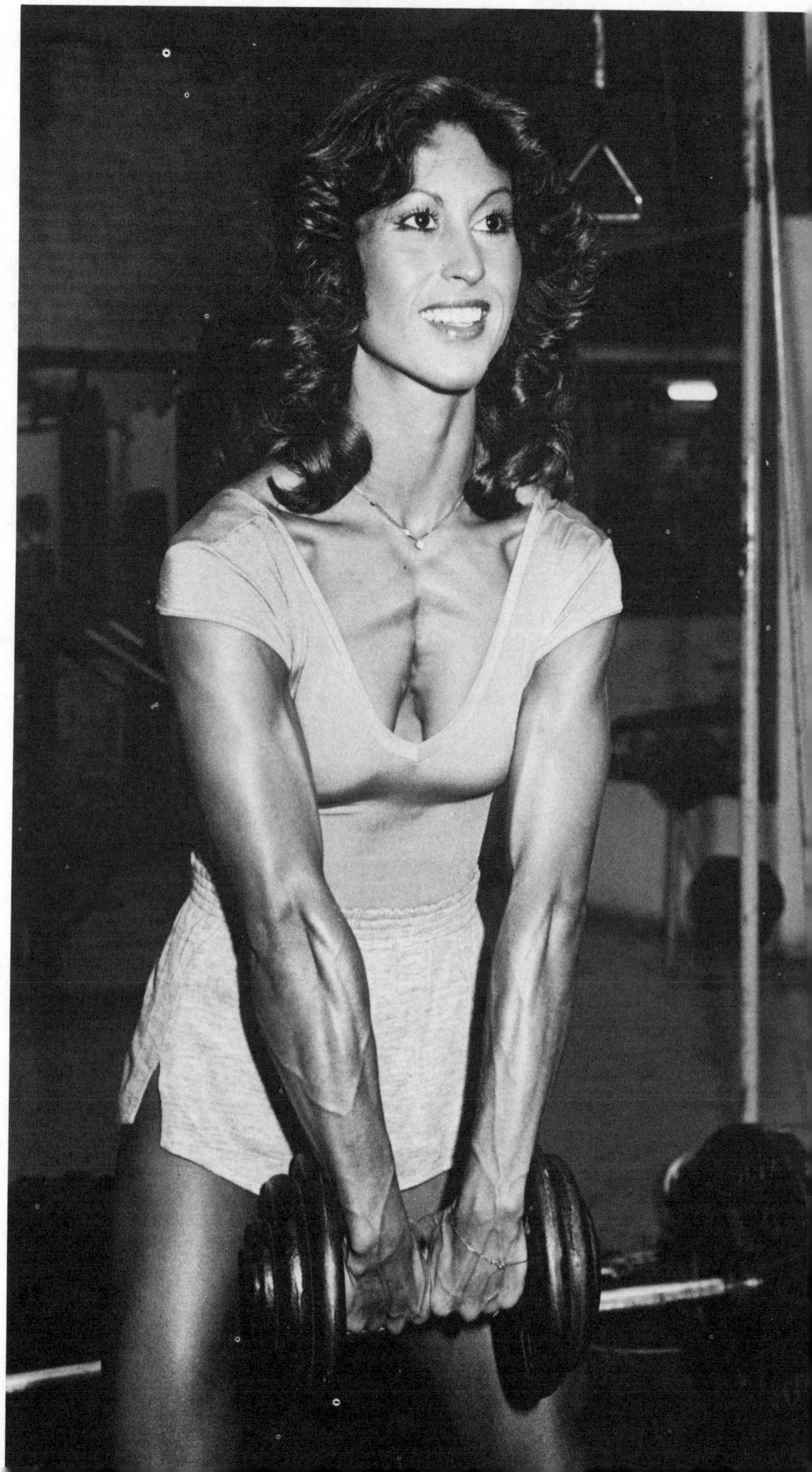

A final source of income from bodybuilding comes from writing books such as this. Unfortunately, the opportunity to sell a book to a national publishing company is limited to those elite women who have both won a prestigious title—or developed a reputation in some other way—and have the ability to write well. Still, for the rare woman who fulfills these requirements, writing a book can be very profitable.

While there are already numerous opportunities for champion pro bodybuilders to make a living from the sport, there will be many more opening up in the future. We predict that by 1985, one or more women bodybuilders will be making over $100,000 per year from the above sources, plus from endorsing exercise equipment and food supplements. Yes, the future of professional women's bodybuilding is bright!

PROFILE OF A CHAMPION

So that you will have a standard against which to compare yourself while you progress as a bodybuilder, we will close this chapter with a profile of Rachel McLish, the greatest woman bodybuilder to date. During 1980, Rachel became both the first amateur U.S. Champion and the first professional Ms. Olympia winner. And by the time you read this profile, she will no doubt have won numerous other top-level competitions.

In 1980, Rachel McLish was a 24-year-old bodybuilder from Harlington, Texas. At 5'6" in height, she weighed 117-118 pounds in her best condition. And at this body weight, she was crisply muscular and had a good degree of muscle mass to compliment her superb body proportions.

By 1980, Rachel McLish had been training hard and consistently with weights for five years and had been interested in physical fitness for most of her life. "My father trains with weights," she recalled recently, "and at 10 I was already mimicking him in his workouts. I literally grew up admiring firm and shapely muscles on both men and women.

"I didn't participate much in sports as a kid, but was deeply involved in dance studies and was a cheerleader in high school. I was never satisfied with just a lithe figure, and always wanted more muscle and strength. Fortunately, my older sister was obsessed with having a great figure—especially a flat stomach—so we were jogging and casually exercising with weights long before those activities became popular with women.

Rachel McLish, a champion from Texas.

"Then in 1975—when I was a sophmore at Pan American University—I began working at a health club, primarily so I could work out there regularly without buying a membership. I have trained hard and consistently ever since, first just for health and fitness, but lately specifically for bodybuilding competition.

Flanked by Joe Weider, left, and Frank Zane, right, Rachel receives her 1980 Ms. Olympia title.

Frank Zane (Mr. Olympia) presents Rachel McLish with her Ms. Olympia trophy.

"Early in 1980, I saw an advertisement for the U.S. Championships held in April that year. I immediately decided to enter the competition and began to intensify my normal four-days-per-week workouts and tighten up my diet. My workout frequency jumped to six days per week, and I worked each muscle group three times per week on a split routine.

"Typically, I did five or six sets of six to eight reps for every body part, using the heaviest weights I could handle with strict form. To build muscle size, my body requires this heavy-weight/low-rep approach, and since muscularity is my strong point, I train rather differently before a competition than most women."

To illustrate precisely how Rachel McLish trains, here is the exact precontest chest routine she used three times per week prior to winning her U.S. Championships:

Rachel holds a compulsory pose during the prejudging at the 1980 Ms. Olympia contest.

1. Machine Flyes: 1 × 6, 35 pounds on each arm
2. Machine Bench Press: 1 × 6, 140 pounds
3. Dumbbell Flyes: 1 × 7–8, 25 pounds each hand
4. Barbell Bench Press: 1 × 6–7, 110 pounds
5. Isometric Pectoral Contractions: one minute

This routine was done one exercise after another in only five or six total minutes, so it is obvious that Rachel prefers to rest very little between sets, even though she uses maximum training poundages in all of her bodybuilding movements.

Rachel's precontest diet stressed a high-protein, low-carbohydrate intake, which is at odds with the more commonly used high-protein, moderate-carbohydrate, low-fat diet most competitive bodybuilders utilize. She ate red meats and averaged 1000–1200 calories per day. Rachel's supplements included milk-and-egg protein powder, multiple vitamins and minerals, and B-complex vitamins.

With this diet and her intense bodybuilding workouts, Rachel maintained her usual body weight of 117–118 pounds as the show approached, but she gained muscle mass and lost fat, which dramatically improved her appearance on stage from the way she looked in the off-season. And Rachel McLish would like to continue her approach to health and fitness for life.

"There's truth in the old adage that beauty comes from the inside out," Ms. McLish maintained. "The bodybuilding life-style—the training, diet, and regular habits—results in buoyant health, which translates into radiant beauty. I always look my best in the sense of feminine beauty on the day of a show when I'm totally peaked out, so I'll still be bodybuilding when I'm 75. And I'll expect to look 39 at that age!"

CONCLUSION

You are now equipped with all of the knowledge you will need to reach your health, appearance and functional goals. The key to your success now becomes *you*. Only you can do the workouts, only you can avoid tempting junk foods, and only you can be sure you put 100 percent into all of your weight training and bodybuilding efforts. But when you do do everything correctly and to the limits of your abilities, *you* are the one who benefits. Go for it!

Appendix:

Answers to Twenty Commonly Asked Questions about Weight Training and Bodybuilding

Q: *What kinds of women lift weights? Weight training seems like an activity that would appeal primarily to students and younger women. What about us housewives?*

A: Actually, a random sample of women who train regularly with weights would be a microcosm of American Society. From 10 to 90 years of age, all kinds of women—from physicians and lawyers to housewives and students—are training with weights. Essentially, weight training is an appropriate physical activity for *any* woman. And regardless of who or what you are, weight training is for *you*!

Q: *Will weight training improve my golf game? I've heard that it will make my body tight and ruin the fluidity of my swing.*

A: Weight training will improve your golf game—as well as your performance in any other sport—by increasing the strength of your muscles. This allows you to hit a golf ball harder, driving it further down the fairway. In the same way, weight training allows you to hit a tennis ball harder, run faster, or jump higher.

Numerous scientific studies have proven that weight training actually increases body flexibility, so you need not worry about becoming tight from it. And as long as you are actively practicing your sport, weight training will strengthen your skeletal muscles to such an extent that you will actually have better manual dexterity for such sports as golf, basketball, and softball.

Q: *I am 56 years of age. Is it too late to benefit from weight training.*

A: No! It is never too late to benefit from progressive weight training and healthy nutritional practices. Your body will respond the same as that of a girl of 16, although perhaps not as quickly. And in the long run—since you started training so late in life—you can't expect to make the same ultimate degree of progress that a 16-year-old girl can make.

You will need to be more cautious in breaking in to training, since you have been out of good physical condition far longer than younger women. It should take you two to three weeks more to get your body used to regular exercise, but once you're into the swing you'll harvest huge benefits from weight training. We know several women in their 70s who are making good progress, and even one who is 82 and enjoying her weight workouts more than most 16-year-old girls!

One of the founders of the Women's Bodybuilding Association and three-time winner of the Miss Eastern United States title, April Nicotra is proof that weight training will not make any woman look like a man.

Q: *Won't weight training ruin my femininity? I'm very fearful that I'll end up looking like a man if I take up weight training!*

A: This is totally untrue, but it's one of the most persistent myths that bodybuilding and weight training has had to endure. To build a man's massive and clearly delineated muscles, you would need to totally change the natural hormonal balances in your body.

While both men and women have estrogen and testosterone in their bodies, women have very high levels of estrogen and men have high levels of testosterone. To build massive muscles, you would need to have a man's levels of testosterone in your body, and you could only achieve such testosterone levels by having it artificially injected into your body. Undoubtedly, this is something no sane woman would consider doing.

Q: *My brother told me that any muscles I develop will turn to fat if I stop working out. He used to lift weights and now he's a fat slob, so I'm inclined to believe him. What is the truth?*

A: Again, this is totally untrue, and it's another one of the myths we have to contend with in weight-training and bodybuilding circles. Essentially, it is physiologically impossible for muscle tissue to turn to fat in the human body. When you stop training with weights, your muscles will gradually shrink back to their original size, with this process taking about as long as it took you to develop the muscle tissue in the first place. "But," we're sure you're thinking, "what about my fat slob of a brother?"

If you fail to watch your diet—whether training with weights or not—you will grow fat. Undoubtedly, your brother eats like a pig, which is why he looks like one. It is *not* because his muscles have turned to fat, which is merely his excuse for being so fat. When he stopped training, his muscles shrank back to their original size, while his poor eating habits added fat to his body.

Q: *Will weight training help me to get rid of the flab on the backs of my upper arms?*

A: If you combine the correct weight training program with a good low-calorie diet, you can eliminate the flab on the backs of your upper arms—or anywhere else on your body—within a few weeks. In your case, a training program stressing triceps exercises will tone the muscle tissues in your problem area, which by itself will result in marked improvement. It will not, however, significantly reduce the fatty deposits lying over the triceps muscles or anywhere else on your body. For this, you must reduce your daily caloric intake, which will progressively reduce fat deposits all over your body and particularly in your problem area. So with time and consistency, your flabby upper arms can definitely regain their youthful firmness.

In 1979, Michigan State University student Patsy Chapman won the "Best in the World" Women's Bodybuilding Championships.

Q: *How soon can I expect to see results from my weight workouts?*

A: In terms of strength development, you can actually see progress following your very first workout. By the time your next training session rolls around, you will find yourself significantly stronger. While you might have had to struggle to Curl 20 pounds six times during your first workout, you'll lift it with ease in your second training session.

You should begin to notice positive changes in your body after only a week or two of training, particularly if you are also on a reduced-calorie diet. Your limbs will become firmer, and your muscles will be harder to the touch, an indication that you're building new muscle tissue. After a month of training, some of your muscles will actually appear larger, and will *be* larger when evaluated with a tape measure.

Q: *I am confined to a wheelchair. Would it benefit me to try a little bodybuilding?*

A: Yes! One of the most neglected—and yet most valuable—facets of weight training is its great value to the disabled. If you are confined to a wheelchair, you can still do a wide variety of weight-training movements for your upper body, either while seated in your chair or lying on your back on a flat exercise bench. Your health and fitness will improve greatly from such exercise, and once you are used to regular workouts, you'll find that they're the most enjoyable part of your day.

Q: *I'd like to start weight training, but I'm afraid of what my husband will think about it. How should I break the news to him?*

A: The best way to let your husband know of your interest in weight training is to have him read this book. Then he'll learn for himself about how much weight training can improve your appearance, health, physical fitness, and strength. Then let him *see* the results. Once he notices how foxy you are beginning to look because of your weight-training workouts, he'll probably want to train along with you to improve his own appearance.

Q: *Will I have to train for life if I begin lifting weights? I don't want to be a slave to my workouts!*

A: No, you don't *have* to continue weight training for life, but you will probably want to! With time, you will find that your weight workouts are the most enjoyable thing you do each

Mandy Tanny was the first female selected to judge an international men's bodybuilding contest.

day. They will relieve your tensions and relax you so completely that you will soon find yourself positively addicted to them for life. Ultimately, you will actually feel physically miserable (or the way "normal" women *always* feel, as opposed to the heightened feeling of well-being you have when weight training regularly) whenever you miss one of your regular workouts!

Q: *Won't weight training injure my back? Lifting such heavy weights simply can't be good for the human body.*

A: If you learn the correct biomechanical positions recommended for each exercise in this book, you will probably never injure your back or any other part of your body while working out with weights. The only ways you will sustain an injury from weight training are to use incorrect biomechanical positions, to not warm up sufficiently, or to neglect using collars on your barbell and spotters when you use heavy weights in a workout.

Q: *Can I train with weights during my menstrual cycle?*

A: You can continue weight training—and all other forms of physical activity—while menstruating. A large number of women have told us that they suffered far fewer menstrual complications (cramps, headaches, depression, etc.) after beginning to weight train and watch their diets.

Q: *Is it appropriate to weight train during a pregnancy?*

A: Weight training can—and *should*—be continued during pregnancy. Scientific studies have shown that physically active women experience far fewer complications from their pregnancies than do less active women. If you continue to weight train (under the supervision of your physician, of course) during your pregnancy, you can expect to experience a shorter and easier labor, and you'll be able to bounce back to your prepregnancy figure in only four to six weeks after giving birth.

Q: *I aspire to a career in acting and modeling. Will weight training help or hurt my chances to become a successful actress and model?*

A: Numerous actresses and models train regularly with weights to tone and improve their bodies, and many more are becoming bodybuilders every week. Raquel Welch is one actress who has weight trained regularly for most of her career, and it's easy to see that weight workouts never did her any harm.

Q: *If I weight train regularly, won't I eat more? It seems inevitable that I will* gain *rather than* lose *weight if I lift weights.*

A: Actually, any kind of vigorous exercise performed regularly will decrease your appetite. And while weight training will inevitably increase your muscle mass, you will tend to lose body weight if you have excessive fat deposits around your body (most women do). At the very least, you will maintain your body weight, as your muscle mass increases at about the same rate as your workouts burn off fat.

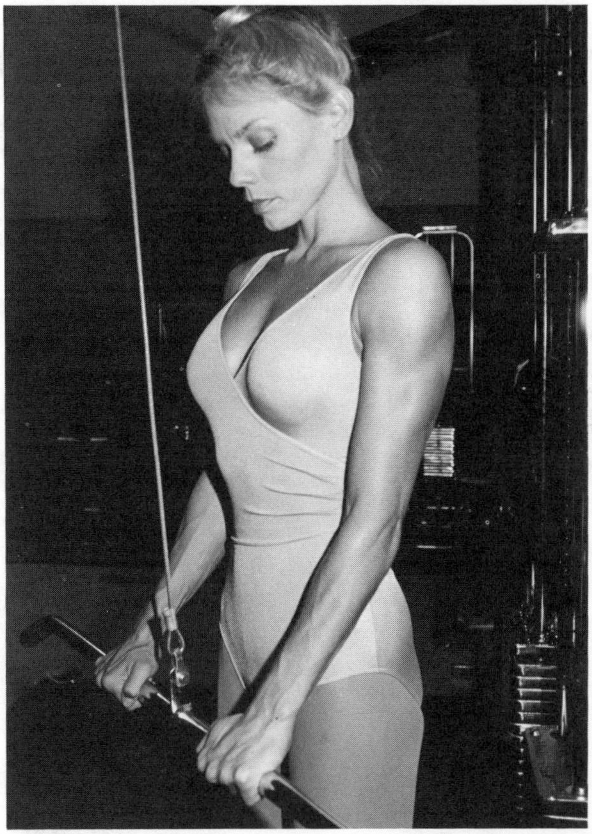

Susie Green, formerly an advertising model, is now a rising star in women's professional bodybuilding.

Q: *I'm very thin and underweight. Can weight training help me?*

A: It definitely can, and we receive numerous testimonials from underweight women who have normalized their appearance by weight training and increasing the amount of food they eat.

Weight training inevitably increases the body's muscle mass, so if you can do this *and* add a little body fat by eating more food, you can gradually normalize your body weight.

Q: *How much time will be required each day if I take up bodybuilding?*

A: You will be able to achieve good results from less than an hour per day three or four times per week. The only way bodybuilding can become excessively time-consuming is when you intend to compete. For the last three to four weeks before a competition you may need to devote up to four or five hours per day to your training, posing practice, and tanning. The rest of the year, however, it should take a competitive bodybuilder no more than one to one-and-a-half hours per day four days a week to get in productive workouts.

Q: *How expensive will it be to take up weight training?*

A: If you invest in an expensive workout suit and a spa membership, it could cost you up to $500 per year to engage in regular weight training. But if you work out at home in a T-shirt and shorts, you can get by easily on an initial investment of only $50, the cost of an inexpensive adjustable barbell set. For as little as $150 to $200, you can completely equip a home gym in your basement, garage, or spare room.

Susie Green works out for 90 minutes in a four-day-per-week split routine which her coach changes every four to six weeks. For aerobic sessions on off-days, she rides a stationary bike for 30 minutes.

Q: *Where will I weight train when I go on my annual vacation trips?*

A: Actually, there are gyms, YMCAs, spas, and Nautilus facilities all over North America, and most offer short-term memberships. If you want to continue working out during your vacation, try one of these.

As an alternative, simply cease training while on your vacation, and resume it when you return home. If you've worked out regularly all year, your body can actually benefit from a one- to three-week layoff from training once a year.

Q: *Will it be necessary to watch my diet if I begin bodybuilding?*

A: No, but you will receive the fastest and best results from weight training and bodybuilding if you also watch your diet. Still, you'll be able to significantly improve your strength, health, and physical appearance by only weight training, even if your diet consists of ice cream and pizza most of the time.

Rachel McLish: "Beauty comes from the inside out."

Glossary

Glossary

Bar—The steel shaft forming the handle of a barbell or dumbbell. The bar of most dumbbells is 12–14 inches long, while barbell bars vary in length from four to seven feet. The weight of this bar must be taken into consideration when adding plates to form a required exercise poundage.

Barbell—Consisting of a bar, sleeve, collars, and plates, this is the basic piece of equipment for weight training. Barbells can be either adjustable (allowing the weights to be changed) or fixed (with the plates welded or otherwise fastened permanently into position).

Bodybuilding—A form of weight training in which the primary objective is to change the form or appearance of one's body. Often bodybuilding can be a competitive sport for both women and men.

Collar—The cylindrical metal fastener that holds barbell or dumbbell plates in position on the bar. There are inside collars and outside collars, both of which are held in position on the bar by a set screw or special clamp.

Dumbbell—This is merely a short-handled barbell which is intended primarily for use in one hand. A dumbbell has all of the other characteristics of a barbell.

Exercise—Each individual movement done in a weight-training program (e.g., a Bench Press or Squat). This is also sometimes called a movement.

Intensity—The amount of actual work done by a muscle or muscles during an exercise or entire workout. Intensity is normally increased by either adding weight to the bar or machine being used, or by increasing the number of repetitions done for an exercise.

Olympic Lifting—The main international form of weight lifting, in which the Snatch and Clean and Jerk are contested to see which athlete can lift the most combined weight in the two exercises.

Plates—The flat cast iron or vinyl-covered concrete discs that are fitted on the ends of a barbell or dumbbell bar to make up the training poundage for a particular exercise.

Powerlifting—A form of competitive weight lifting in which the Squat, Bench Press, and Deadlift are performed to see which athlete can lift the most combined weight in the three exercises. While some women compete with men in Olympic lifting, powerlifting is an organized women's sport with National and World Championships held each year and regularly broadcast on national television.

Repetition—Each individual complete cycle of an exercise (e.g., the full bending and straightening of the arms in a Bench Press). This term is often abbreviated to rep. Normally several repetitions (usually six to twelve) are done of each exercise in a training program.

Routine—The complete program of exercises done on an individual training day. This is also called a program or a schedule.

Set—A distinct grouping of repetitions in a particular exercise (usually six to twelve), after which a trainee takes a rest interval of 30 to 90 seconds, followed by additional sets of the same movement.

Sleeve—The hollow metal tube fitted over the bar of an adjustable barbell or dumbbell. This sleeve helps the bar to rotate more easily in the hands during an exercise. To aid a trainee to grip the bar when her hands are sweaty, this sleeve is usually scored with shallow cross-hatched grooves called knurlings.

Weight Lifting—A form of weight training in which athletes compete in weight classes to see who can lift the most combined weight in either the two Olympic lifts (Snatch and Clean and Jerk) or the three power lifts (Squat, Bench Press, and Deadlift). The weight classes now used in international competition are 52 kg. (114½ lbs.), 56 kg. (123½ lbs.), 60 kg. (132¼ lbs.), 67½ kg. (148¾ lbs.), 75 kg. (165¼ lbs.), 82½ kg. (181¾ lbs.), 90 kg. (198¼ lbs.), 100 kg. (220½ lbs.), 110 kg. (242½ lbs.), and unlimited (over 110 kg.).

Weight Training—A form of physical exercise using weight resistance provided by barbells, dumbbells, or exercise machines. Weight training can be pursued toward numerous goals—bodybuilding, improving sports performance, increasing strength, competing as a weight lifter, gaining weight, slimming, rehabilitating an injury, increasing aerobic conditioning, improving health, providing a greater sense of personal well-being, etc.

Workout—The program or routine of exercises done to its completion each training day. This is also called a training session.

Recommended Reading

BOOKS

Anatomy

Gray, Henry, *Anatomy, Descriptive and Surgical,* London: Crown Publishers, 1968.

Flexibility

Anderson, Bob, *Stretching,* Fullerton, Calif.: Anderson, 1975

Nutrition

Nutrition Almanac, New York: McGraw-Hill Book Co., 1975.

Physiology

Astrand, Per-Olof and Rodahl, Kaare, *Textbook of Work Physiology,* New York: McGraw-Hill Book Co., 1977.

Weight Training and Bodybuilding

Barrilleaux, Doris and Murray, Jim, *Inside Weight Training for Women,* Chicago: Contemporary Books, 1978.

Columbu, Franco with Fels, George, *Winning Bodybuilding,* Chicago: Contemporary Books, 1977.

Darden, Ellington, *The Nautilus Book,* Chicago: Contemporary Books, 1980.

Dobbins, Bill and Sprague, Ken, *The Gold's Gym Weight Training Book,* Los Angeles: J. P. Tarcher, Inc., 1978.

Kennedy, Robert, *Natural Body Building for Everyone,* New York: Sterling Publishing Co., Inc., 1980.

Lance, Kathryn, *Getting Strong,* Indianapolis/New York: The Bobbs-Merrill Company, Inc., 1978.

Leen, Edie, *Complete Women's Weight Training Guide,* Mountain View, Calif.: Anderson World, Inc., 1980.

Mentzer, Mike with Friedberg, Andy, *The Mentzer Method to Fitness,* New York: William Morrow and Company, Inc., 1980.

Murray, Jim, *Inside Bodybuilding,*, Chicago: Contemporary Books, 1978.

Murray, Jim, *Inside Weight Lifting and Weight Training*, Chicago: Contemporary Books, 1977.

Reynolds, Bill, *Complete Weight Training Book,* Mountain View, Calif.: Anderson World, Inc., 1976.

Schwarzenegger, Arnold with Hall, Douglas Kent, *Arnold's Bodyshaping for Women*, New York: Simon and Schuster, 1979.

Sing, Vanessa, *Lift for Life!*, New York: Bolder Books, 1977.

Sprague, Ken, *The Gold's Gym Book of Strength Training for Athletes,* Los Angeles: J. P. Tarcher, Inc., 1979.

Weider, Joe, *The IFBB Album of Bodybuilding All-Stars,* New York: Hawthorn Books, Inc., 1979.

Zane, Frank and Christine, *The Zane Way to a Beautiful Body,* New York: Simon and Schuster, 1979.

MAGAZINES

Muscle & Fitness and *Shape* are the world's leading bodybuilding and self-improvement magazines. A year's subscription to *Muscle & Fitness* is $24.00 and to *Shape* it is $20.00, both from Weider Health and Fitness, Inc., 21100 Erwin Street, Woodland Hills, CA 91367. Both magazines are also available on all newsstands.

Index